CW01263140

LOSE YOUR CRITIC
FOR GOOD

PALMETTO
PUBLISHING
Charleston, SC
www.PalmettoPublishing.com

Copyright © 2024 by Sue Erhart

All rights reserved

No portion of this book may be reproduced, stored in a retrieval system, or transmitted in any form by any means–electronic, mechanical, photocopy, recording, or other–except for brief quotations in printed reviews, without prior permission of the author.

Hardcover ISBN: 979-8-8229-5190-7
Paperback ISBN: 979-8-8229-5191-4
eBook ISBN: 979-8-8229-5192-1

LOSE YOUR CRITIC FOR GOOD

A Step-by-Step Process for
Reclaiming Your Spirit

SUE ERHART

To Zack, Ada, and Jacob

PREFACE

I spent many years with a critic who I had no idea was living for free in my head. I had grown so accustomed to the critic that we unwittingly went on a journey together, which I thought was the only way through life. The critic stomped around and told me what was wrong, missing, or out of place, and I did my best to meet its requirements. It wasn't an arrangement I planned; it was simply how I thought life was supposed to be.

Then I discovered my true self under all the mistaken ideas that the critic concocted. I found that strong inner voice that comes forward in life to say *enough*. Enough with the ways of a critic, who is nothing more than an idea based in fear.

My own journey to shake myself loose from the critic was years in the making. I simply had no guide for how to do this work. Instead I set out to rely on my inner wisdom and my strong belief in a power higher than me to help me dismantle this habit of thought that seemed to skew negative. And in that work, I found myself.

My own critic was so well established that I thought it was me. I thought the incessant messages of what was wrong were a core part of my own being and not a thought pattern that could be interrupted. I thought the critic was the key to my success in life.

With hindsight, I can now see that the critic fortified me to take a stand for my own true self, and my own inner goodness, in a way that is supercharged. I was so adept at tuning out the critic that I no longer noticed when it was yammering on in the background. I simply accepted the noisiness as part of life and not something I could affect.

If I could return to my younger days, I would tell myself that critical thought patterns are unnecessary, unhelpful, and likely to cause anxiety, fear, and worry. I'd counsel my younger self to take a stand for her true self and to do the work of breaking free of the critic now, before the critic became part of the fabric of her life. I'd carefully guide myself toward a new way of thinking and seeing so I could thrive in every area of life. I wrote this book for me as much as I have written it for you.

The irony of my entire story is this: I thought the critic was the part of me who was aligned with spirit. I thought my critical thought patterns were the result of a desire to be good. I thought the ideas that spurred me to criticize myself emanated from my own soul. As if I were doing God's work by keeping tabs on everything that could, or did, go wrong.

Now that I am on the other side of that thinking, it's hard for me to believe I had it so wrong. It's hard for me to appreciate how ingrained these ideas are in our culture, our society, and our religions. And it's hard for me to offer you any advice for losing your critic unless you are willing to see your own true nature—your spirit—as the best thing going on.

If I could go back in time, I'd tell my younger self that if she could listen to her own spirit instead of the noisy chatter of the critic, she'd live a life that exceeded all her expectations. I'd tell her that the key to success in life was her indominable spirit—which has grown strong in reaction to the critic—and that the critic was only a diversion keeping her from what she truly wanted. I'd tell her that the spirit-led life is more fun, more interesting, and way more fruitful than following along with the critic's directives.

And because I can't go back, I'm paying it forward. I'm sharing my best advice so you can see your thought patterns and make a better choice. I'm getting the message out on behalf of all the souls so that we can collectively move past our belief that self-criticism is holy, necessary, or good. I'm out here on the front lines, dealing with my critic when it flares up, and then sending back messages to those who want to live a life of power.

That's what a spirit-led life is to me. A life full of power, confidence, clarity, and joy. A life of abundance, excitement, satisfaction, and love. A life of good ideas, infinite inspiration, and frivolous fun. A life that unfolds rather than drives for results.

Five years ago, I was doing little writing. Three years ago, I was recovering from a trauma that set me back and caused me to question everything I knew. One year ago, this book was not even in my purview. Yet, in hindsight, I can see every little decision that led to where I am today, and I can say with certainty that my spirit guided me each day. It wasn't hard. It wasn't a battle. It wasn't even planned. It simply unfolded over the course of a few years.

My point is this: your critic will tell you that the spirit-led life is the worse choice. The critic will suggest that a meandering path is a waste of time. Your critic will drown out your inner wisdom if you allow it to continue.

Take a stand for yourself and prepare to lose the critic. For good.

CONTENTS

Preface vii
Introduction 1
Day 1   Releasing the Critic 7
Day 2   Reasons for the Critic 15
Day 3   Innate Worthiness 23
Day 4   Worthiness Applied 32
Day 5   Heal Your Past 39
Day 6   Unconditional Love 47
Day 7   Go Easy 54
Day 8   Micro-Meditations 60
Day 9   Mirror Work 67
Day 10 Your Words Matter 74
Day 11 Perfection of Today 82
Day 12 Life Without the Critic 90
Day 13 Use a Logbook 97
Day 14 Own Your Day 104
Day 15 Embrace the Lull 111
Day 16 Clear the Blocks 119

Day 17	Crafting a Turnaround	126
Day 18	Leverage the Backlash	134
Day 19	Find Your Why	141
Day 20	Compare to Know	149
Day 21	Notice in Neutral	157
Day 22	Saying *I want*	164
Day 23	Emotions	171
Day 24	Open Your Heart	178
Day 25	Daydreams as Tools	183
Day 26	Intuitive Next Actions	190
Day 27	Art of Allowing	198
Day 28	Soothing Self-Talk	205

Conclusion 213

Postscript 216

About the Author 219

INTRODUCTION

Trust is a two-way street. When you learn to trust yourself, you gain exponentially. That's because you are on both sides of the equation. You trust you, which begets more trust in you.

I learned to trust myself one day at a time when I stopped doing what others expected of me and started doing whatever the hell I wanted to do. And I found that my biggest enemy was me.

My own mind had fabricated all these rules about how I was supposed to live my life, and those rules turned into a nasty critic who always saw lack. The critic was the first to notice what was wrong. The critic was the first to plan for things to go haywire. The critic was great at telling me how I screwed up.

The critic was so good at this that I hardly noticed the negativity. When I perseverated over one missed step, I thought I was being careful and avoiding future errors. When I couldn't take my mind off a perceived slight, I thought I was seeking peace with another. And when I would tell myself, over and over, that what I had in life was enough, I thought I was being prudent and good.

A critic isn't just a naysayer. It's the idea that says, *This is good enough*. It's the patterns of thought that make you settle for less and then wonder why you are bored. It's the part of you that says, *Don't take a risk; what we have is enough*. The critic is a habit of thought that keeps you small.

I kicked my critic to the curb by doing mindset work, practicing affirmations, and watching my thinking. I worked at this project for a couple of years because I was tired of the incessant chatter, judging, and shaming that my own mind heaped on me. And in that work, I found my calling.

Losing a critic is a project of epic proportions. That's because no part of your life is unaffected by a critic. Every part of your life must be reseen to heal the wounds the critic inflicts. The path to freedom from a critic is not an exercise, a project, or a program. It's a way of living. And it's a way of living that will not only free you of the critic but also set you up to soar toward any life goal you choose.

The critic is an idea. Rightly stated, it's an amalgamation of ideas that seem to coalesce into a chatterbox who tells you what's wrong. What's off. What is out of place. As an idea, however, the critic can be dismantled, destroyed, and depowered to no longer have a say in your life. I know because I am now living life critic-free.

I still have limiting beliefs and mistaken ideas, which I deal with as they come up, but I am now living life on the positive side of the ledger, rather than wallowing in lack based on the critic's malfeasance.

And if I can do this, so can you.

Your desire to lose your critic is a desire to nurture. Your realization that criticism never provides long-term motivation is the *aha* that you need to embrace a new way of living. Your own interest in a life free of a critic is the best indication that this book is for you.

Critics are pervasive because we share a common limiting belief that it's better to "face the truth" of our failings to gain long-term success. Yet science has shown, over and over, how positive reinforcement leads to true success. We all know that the carrot is the better motivator than the stick, yet we allow our critics free reign in our minds and in our lives.

Critics are no one's fault. But they are your responsibility. To manage, to take down, and to rebuild if you want to live the life you were meant to lead. No person chooses life with a critic, but many of us fail to stop the critic because we think "that's just how we are."

Not true. Your true essence is a being created in love. Which is the opposite of a critic. Your essence is powered by activities you love, not by deconstructing every activity you engage in. The true you—the soul without the critic—only speaks in the language of love: I want, I desire, and I'm interested.

And therein lies the problem most of us face with our critics. We think the critic is our soul, come to show us our failings so we can repent. Not true. But that's the reason I see for so many tolerating a critic who they know is not helpful.

This book will challenge you to rethink everything in your life, and everything you know about why you have allowed this critic to rule your life. It will urge you to monitor your thinking to see where your patterns of thought cause you problems, and it will encourage you to welcome in your own spirit to disassemble your critic for good. The critic has the upper hand today because you are unaware of what your soul sounds like if you have a habit of listening to your critic. Once you break that habit, however, your spirit has all the power to guide you toward what you love.

In this book, we will explore all the ways the critic shows up. Some are obvious; some will surprise you. Together, we'll build a positive sense of self so you can fight off the critic from a place of strength. As we do so, we'll uncover our own limiting beliefs and mistaken ideas that play into the critic's routines. And by the end, we'll create a new routine to help you do this work on your own.

What I want to impress upon you is this: the critic is a habit of thought. Nothing more. And if you can create a habit of thought that criticizes, then you have the power to create a habit of thought that heals, uplifts, and energizes every part of your life. If the critic can exist, so can the uplifter. If the critic can get airtime, so can your inner voice of love. If the critic can get your attention, so too can an idea that makes you feel alive.

Your critic isn't a problem. It's an opportunity. And I am going to show you, step-by-step, how to unlock the power of your critic so you can use it to better your own life.

What's the end result? Confidence. Clarity. A sense of purpose. Unconditional self-love. Goals for days. You arrive at the end of your journey, whole, complete, and ready to live life on your terms. And best of all: you trust yourself.

I will guide you, but you are the one who will show up to do the work of reclaiming your mind as your own. And in so doing, you'll establish a relationship of trust so strong that even the stray negative thought or setback won't cause you concern. Instead, it will become an interesting tidbit in the life that is yours.

Our work together will be broken down by chapters and days. I recommend that you read one chapter in a day and do the work assigned. This will allow you to obtain the maximum benefit from this work. If you prefer to read ahead, read the whole book and then come back to do one chapter at a time for best results.

Our minds need time to assimilate new ideas, which is why I recommend this pacing. It also provides ample opportunities to apply what you are learning in your daily life. Trust me; you want to get to the other side with this work, so it's worth the slow progression.

You are worthy of life without a critic. You are worthy of a life that eschews second-guessing and uncertainty loops. You are worthy of positive, uplifting ideas that help you accomplish your goals. You are worthy of being loved. My perspective naturally is affected by my own beliefs, so I won't be shy in revealing how I think. You, however, are the decider of what you choose to believe. I hope you use your power of choice to take a stand for the true you and lose the critic for good. I did, and I am reaping the benefits even as I write this book.

I am no expert on the human mind. But I am now an expert on my own mind. You will be too once you complete this book.

You will see your own mind as a tool that can be leveraged to help you. You will realize that your ultimate freedom is the power you hold over your own mind. You will come to understand that thoughts hold power, but not if we take it away from them.

We will dethrone your critic together, and then we will resurrect your own spirit to take its place. And we'll do that with a sense of fun, adventure, and determination. Together.

My own journey is interwoven in these lessons, and I too am walking and re-walking a path to a life of critic-less days. I write as much for me as I do for you. What I do consistently, however, is show up every day for myself and seek to put the critic away. With love.

The critic may be a part of me, but it is no longer in charge. I am. And in the coming chapters, you will learn how powerful it is to set the agenda for your life without a critic telling you to watch out, play small, or go slow. Your first order of business is to set an intention for this work. Here is mine: I intend to show up for myself every day to do the work of losing my critic for good. Your next order of business is to get a notebook and write out your intention at the top of the first page.

LOSE YOUR CRITIC FOR GOOD

This notebook, and my words, will become your traveling companions for this journey. If you are inclined, welcome your own spirit into your journey, and watch yourself grow in power and success for this work.

Day 1

RELEASING THE CRITIC

The ways in which a critic takes hold of your life are nefarious, insidious, and odious. All at the same time. Our work is to notice the critic, which often reveals our limiting beliefs. A limiting belief is any idea that keeps you from accessing the true you. The you on the inside. The you who is ready to break free and soar.

The first limiting belief to tackle is the one that says that the critic is you. That the critic is part of your persona that can't be overcome. That the critic is a fact of life.

These ideas, which are born of our own experience living with a critic, are blocks to removing the critic. We will work together to remove these blocks. To remove a block, you set an intention to let go of the block, and then you seek out a new idea to replace the limiting idea you let go. Notice. Release. Choose. That's it.

Some blocks seem to dissipate the moment we notice them. We identify the block, which is nothing more than an idea, and we conclude that the idea is false, unhelpful, or past its prime. With that noticing, we immediately reject the idea and move to a new belief. This is often done so quickly that we don't see the work. Let's use an example.

If I told you that all people are short, you would hear that idea, reject that idea, and, in your head, think, *People come in all sorts of heights*. All in a millisecond when you aren't aware of what you are doing. We do this as we stumble upon new ideas. Some of them get rejected by us immediately, and we move on.

Your critic has been with you a long time, so you likely have limiting beliefs—blocks—that you aren't seeing. For those, we need to take the time to notice, release, and choose in order to break down the old pattern of thought. And the biggest block I have encountered is the idea that the critic just *is*.

The critic is a habit. A pattern of thought you use to feel safe, superior, or at peace. That's OK. There are good reasons that many of us create a critical pattern of thought. Your first work, however, is to break down the idea that the critic is to be accepted as part of your life.

To do this, I recommend you first try writing. Writing helps the mind see ideas on paper, which makes them more tangible. Writing also slows us down so we can more easily process, or pick apart, the blocks. Writing also provides a record and a reminder of the ideas we are losing and the new ones we are creating.

The foundation of this entire book is one idea: you can choose what you think. By practicing the art of noticing, releasing, and choosing, we deliberately create a new pattern of thought that will serve as the foundation of a critic-free life. We will go slowly, at first, but over time, this process will become second nature. You will spot a block, dismiss it, and seek a better thought, without so much as a pause in your conversation. For today, however, we go step-by-step to seal in this new practice.

In your notebook, write out the idea: *I can't get rid of the critic.* Or *I am a critical person.* Or *I must accept my critic.* I want you to use words that resonate with you, so I will often give you options to suggest different ways of expressing the same idea. Your work is to choose the words that sound most like you. You could write, *I have a critical mind, and that's just how I am.* Or you could write, *I like my critic, and she's helping me succeed.* Pick an idea that feels true for you and write it down.

Look at that idea. Is that idea helpful? Is it true? Could you open yourself to believe a different idea? I personally have no patience for any idea that is not helpful to my life goals, so I am aggressive at ferreting out blocks and swapping them for better ideas. If you are reading this book, then you are likely ready to let go of the idea that you need a critic, or that the critic is you. If you are ready, set an intention to let go of the idea that the critic must be accepted as a part of life.

To set an intention, you use your mind. You look at that idea on the page and you think—deliberately—that you are ready to release that idea so you can create space for a better idea. I like to visualize this process as thought clouds that exist around me. When I release an idea, it floats away, thus creating space for a new idea that I want in my life. I see the release of an idea as a powerful spiritual practice that emanates from my core essence. It's me deciding that a thought is not worthy of my life. So I let it go.

At first, you might say out loud, *I release this thought.* Or *I am ready to let go of this old idea.* Or *I want to free this idea from my experience.* The words are irrelevant. What matters is your intention to say, *I no longer want this idea, I no longer believe this idea, and I am ready for a better idea to take its place.*

Now for the fun part. We choose a better idea. I get excited for this part, and often overshoot what I am ready to believe, so I will walk you through a process of choosing an idea that helps you move in the direction you want to go.

In this case, we want to create a new idea that the critic can be lost. That the critic can go away. That the critic is a habit of thought that we can change. I already believe that, so my new idea would be: *the critic is wholly unnecessary for life*. You might not be there yet, so seek out an idea or combination of words that seems true to you. Such as *I could lose the critic*. Or *I am interested in learning more about a critic-less life*. Or *The critic could be a problem*. As with all cases, use words that feel good to you. Use words that uplift you or give you a jolt of positive feedback. Choose new ideas that you want to be true.

As I said, I often overshoot with my new ideas and head toward the statements that I want to be true. I am now adept at jumping to new ideas and seizing them to benefit my life. You, however, are just starting out and may need to "ladder up" to get to a belief that you too can lose your critic.

"Laddering up" is my term for linking a series of thoughts together to get you to a new idea. You start with an idea that you can swallow and then improve it, rung by rung, until you get to a place where you want to be.

If you started with *I could lose the critic*, your next rung could be *And I am ready to lose the critic*, and then the next rung would be *The critic isn't necessary*, and then the next would be *The critic can be overcome*. It's the equivalent of talking yourself into a new idea, often starting with the idea of a *could*.

As in, *I could believe that. I could see that. I could be open to a new idea.*

Once you select a new idea to replace the one you released, write down your new idea. I like to cross out the old one and write the new one nearby. This is a great visual to reinforce that we no longer believe the old idea and that we are working up a belief in a new idea.

Beliefs are formed in many ways. Often, the best way to believe something new is to experience something new. Unfortunately, you have been living with the critic so long that it's unlikely that you will spontaneously lose the critic. Instead, you need to practice these new ideas to dismantle the hold that the critic has on you.

To practice, we say the new idea out loud. We write the new idea over and over. We stand in front of a mirror and rehearse the new idea until it sticks.

Your primary work throughout this book will be to practice new ideas. When you do the work, you create a new belief. And when you create a new belief, you open yourself to new possibilities. Your work is to create a list of new ideas that replace your blocks, and then to practice the new ideas every day until you feel like they are set.

The practice feels weird at first. You won't like looking at yourself in the mirror. You'll feel strange rehearsing new ideas. You might even skip the work because it feels too new.

Here is what I want you to know. You are practicing ideas every moment of every day. Your mind is mostly reaching for old ideas and old, practiced thoughts as you go about your day. All we are doing is gently creating new pathways of ideas that are helpful to your life. So, either you practice new ideas, or you get stuck in old ways of thinking. I hope this motivates you to practice.

I now practice often. Sometimes I use a mirror, and sometimes I just talk to myself while I am driving and say new ideas. I also use notes to remind me of new ideas and place them around my workspace. Once you become adept at taking on new ideas, nothing can stop you. See, then, this valuable practice as a new way of living that harnesses the power of your own mind to be on your side.

That's how I felt about my critic. I felt like my mind was betraying me. I felt like I had no choice but to listen to the criticism. I thought I was doing good work by constantly seeking to improve myself. What I found, however, is that a cycle of trying to improve yourself to prove you are worthy leads to a life where you constantly need to improve yourself to prove you are worthy. Once I hopped off that train of thought, I found an inner worthiness that was conditioned on nothing. Which left the critic with free time, as I no longer listened to any idea that suggested I needed to work harder, do more, or become a better person. I decided that I was enough. And then I got busy dealing with my critic, one thought at a time.

Your work today is to notice, release, and choose a new idea for one of your blocks. Write it out, set your intention, and then choose a new thought. Then practice that new thought as you go about your day. Do it once in front of a mirror. Write the new thought as often as you want. Have fun with this.

You are embarking on a journey to set your spirit free. That's all that's happening. The critic is a block to your own alignment, and once we jostle the critic loose, your spirit will take over and do the rest. Trust me; you are in good hands.

Typical blocks that keep us shackled to a critic, inadvertently:

We think the critic is our soul or inner voice.
We think criticism is necessary to make ourselves do hard things.
We think the critic is us.
We assume that the critic is a default setting and not changeable.
We see the critic as the key to our success.
We enjoy the critic when it is pointed at other people.
We fear complacency if we stop listening to the critic.
We fear imperfection if we stop listening to the critic.
We are unaware of the critic as a critic.

TAKEAWAYS

- You have the resources inside you to see why you have adopted a critic mentality.
- You can notice, release, and choose for any idea that you are carrying.
- Your blocks are simply ideas that are contrary to the truth of who you are.
- Setting your spirit free is a good and worthy goal.

Toby wakes up each morning, sees the alarm clock, and groans. *I can't believe I have to get up now for school.* He trudges to the bathroom, already on autopilot, and takes care of his morning routine. By the time he is zipping up his trousers, his mind is already on the group project he must finish by Friday and how no one but him is putting in the work. He grabs his laptop and his bag and runs for the subway, all the while thinking, *I wish it was Friday.* He arrives at the platform just in time to see the train pulling up. He checks his watch and breathes a sigh of relief: he'll be on time today. He looks around at his fellow passengers as he boards and wonders, *Is anyone happy in the morning?*

Toby's critic is the idea that his life is not what he wants, that his life is in the hands of unseen forces, and that his life is meant to be difficult. Toby would benefit greatly from reframing his critic and then tuning in to his own true self.

Day 2

REASONS FOR THE CRITIC

Your own adventure in losing your critic is about to begin. So now is the perfect time to stop, reflect, and thank the critic for what it has done in your life.

The critic exists for a good reason, just like all facets of life. The goodness of your own soul means that all your creations carry that same goodness. What we will explore are the ways in which the critic has helped us, so we can loosen the hold that these ideas have on us.

Most of us keep a critic because we believe the critic is helpful. Yesterday we dealt with the idea that the critic was essential, or necessary, to your life, and we softened that belief. Today let's soften the idea that the critic is needed for you to succeed. To do that, let's address all the ways that we think that the critic helps us, and then let go of those ideas.

Some of us believe that, if left to our own devices, we would become lazy slugs who did nothing all day but eat and consume content. This is an idea that the critic created, so be mindful that its goals are not the same as your goals. The critic's goal is singular: to keep you safe. The critic just has twisted ideas of what is required for you to be safe.

The critic believes that you are not capable of running your life, accomplishing your goals, and doing activities you love. And the critic believes this because you have relied on fear and criticism to motivate you, as a habit. You work toward others' deadlines but not your own. You do activities because you fear being left out, not because you want to. You create patterns of thought that say, *I need someone else to hold me accountable, or I won't accomplish anything.*

To add to the mix, you are so accustomed to being motivated by fear that you sorta forgot what it means to be motivated by love.

When a person is motivated by love, she does what she loves. She undertakes actions she enjoys. She is interested in life. She has ideas and moves toward them because she wants to. She may not be in love with every part of her life (yet), but there are aspects of every day that she enjoys, savors, and relishes. She uses her good feelings to propel her into action and finds that when she leans into fun, excitement, or joy, good things come her way.

That's the life that the critic is hiding from you.

A critic is a fear. It's a fear that if you love yourself too much, something bad will happen. It's a fear that if you celebrate your good qualities, someone will knock you off your perch. It's a fear that if you allow your true essence to show, people will not love you. And it's a fear that is ready to be dismantled.

Living a life that is motivated by fear is no way to live. If you have a habit of fulfilling everyone else's needs before your own, then you are living in fear. If you have a habit of withholding self-approval until you do hard or right actions, then you are motivated by fear, not love. And if you have a habit of downplaying your natural strengths, then you are a fearmonger who needs to come into the light.

Motivating yourself based on fear is a short-term fix that is never sustainable in the long term. It might cause you to act, to prepare, or to improve, but always at the cost of your own spirit. It's as if you are trading in task completion for the keys to your soul. You would rather do what someone else expects of you than stand tall and proud and say, *This is who I am*. This is not a judgment, or even a blaming session. It's an effort to help you see where you are using fear to move ahead when you could be using love.

That's the real cost of the critic: a missed opportunity to be motivated by love. To do what you love. To be in love with your life. To love being who you are, no strings attached.

A person with a strong critic may not believe that a life motivated by doing what she loves is possible. He may be so convinced by his own critical thoughts that other people can do what they love, but not him. He may even be so entrenched that he lies to himself and says, *I love what I am doing, meeting others' needs before my own*.

To make a shift out of fear and into love, you must open the door to this new idea: a life motivated by love is better than a life motivated by fear. The critic has gotten us this far in life, and for that, we are grateful. But we are now ready to engage with the rest of our life by being motivated by love most of the time.

We learned yesterday the idea of a practice of new ideas. In your notebook, create a page that you call The Practice. Under that heading, write these new ideas:

I can work toward a life that is motivated by doing what I love.

I am open to being motivated by love instead of fear.

I have a great sense of what it means to do something I love.

These new ideas, once you practice them out loud and in front of a mirror, will help you notice things you love that are already in your life. If you have self-care rituals that make you feel good, put attention toward them and savor them to prolong them. If you have a hobby you enjoy, lean into that hobby, and say, *I am doing this activity because I enjoy it.* And if you have any part of your life that you are excited about, go all in thinking about, planning, and enjoying that excitement.

If you need examples, here are a few:

A person who loves washing his car on the weekend could get into that and self-talk during the process, saying, *I love seeing this car get clean. This makes me feel great. I am doing this for free and for me because I enjoy the process and the outcome.*

A person who enjoys food could, with each meal, notice how good the food looks and smells and then savor each bite, saying, *I love eating and the joy it brings to my life. Food is something I love.*

A person who has a penchant for numbers and spreadsheets could, while at work, celebrate a balanced account or get excited about a new way of seeing the data. She could prolong those moments by saying, *This is something I enjoy. I want more feelings of satisfaction like this.*

A person who can't stop weeding his garden could notice his obsession and say, *This work makes me feel wonderful. I feel good pulling weeds. I am doing this because it feels good to me.*

Be open-minded, and look at your entire day. Where can you notice that you are motivated by doing what you love? Do you love a good cup of coffee? Savor it. Do you love a hot shower? Say so. Do you love when the socks all match in the laundry? Celebrate it.

We are pulling on two ends of the spectrum here. We are opening your mind to see that fear is not a good way to live, so that you can open the door to be motivated by love. Then, we are bolstering your belief in your own power to be motivated by what you love.

Before you fly too far ahead of me—we aren't talking about switching careers, leaving a spouse, or moving cross-country to create a life you love. We are talking about you, exactly where you are today, finding any moment that you are loving and seeing that as the direction you want to head. We all want to add in more moments, each day, doing what we love. See yourself as a collector of ideas that motivate you in a positive way.

Do you love order? Are you turned on by taking risk? Do you feel a surge of excitement every time you do something new? Those are all ideas to capture, as they signify an activity you love. I would write these down in my notebook, under the heading *Things That Get Me Going*, and seek to add to that every day. My personal list includes a great cup of coffee, delicious food, comfortable and stylish clothes, and people I get to love. I see each entry as a tiny window into the soul that is me.

For today's work, I encourage you to start small. You aren't looking for your next big career (yet). We are looking for tiny moments when you enjoy life. Tiny moments when you take action because you enjoy what you do, not because you are meeting others' expectations of you. Tiny moments you can add to your day to upend the pendulum that has swung over to the fear side of the ledger.

Life is a balance. When you have too many activities that are all fear-based (you don't want to do them but feel like you must or should), then you lose energy, feel fatigued, and get low. The solution is to add, in tiny steps that often go unnoticed by the critic, to your already-full day. An extra-long shower or bath. Getting your nails done. Reading a fantastic book. Any activity that makes you feel good is what you are reaching for here.

If you try to add in too many feel-good activities, your critic may shout:

You are being lazy.

You aren't producing any income with this.

You will lose your edge if you take your eye off the ball.

None of which is true, but it's what critics all around the world say to keep you safe. When my critic flares, and it still does from time to time, I say, *Thanks for trying to keep me safe, but I know what is best for me.* I know that if I move toward activities I love, I am better able to stand up to a critic, dismantle a critic, and enjoy my life on my terms. All of which are my personal goals.

When you are ready to accept that love is a better motivator than fear, then your critic dissipates. The hold it has on you is based on your mistaken belief that fear is the best motivator. In my book, fear does not stand a chance when there is love to be had.

If you want to delve deeper, journal for ten minutes about a time when you did an activity where the time passed quickly. Where the day flew by. Where you were feeling strong, confident, and carefree. Let that journal entry be a reminder that you do know how to be motivated by love and that you are open to more days like this in your future.

Your critic wasn't created in a day. It won't go away in a day. It will, however, go silent and become more manageable as you take back your power from the beliefs that prop up the critic. That's what we are doing, day by day. Unplugging the power source that is you from the idea that is the critic. Take back that power, and use it to add activities that you love to your day.

Exercise: Write out every way you think the critic has helped you. How it caused you to get up at 5:00 a.m. for a workout. How it caused you to rethink your move cross-country. How it kept you from making a fool of yourself. Write out each reason that comes to mind, as these are the reasons that anchor the critic in your life. Thank the critic. Now, release each of your underlying beliefs and say, *I am ready to allow love to motivate me instead of fear.*

TAKEAWAYS

- Your critic isn't you; it's just an idea of how you think you are supposed to be.
- Learning to lean into activities you love is the antithesis of a critic-led life. Opt for love.
- Your critic will go away if you stay aware and intend to lose the critic.

Veronica is trying to make this delivery for the third time, and these people are never home. *People in posh homes are never home,* she thinks. *Wasting this beautiful house, likely out running around in their fancy car,* she muses. Veronica decides that despite the rules against it, she is going to leave the package without waiting for a signature. *Screw them,* she thinks. *If this package gets stolen, they can simply buy another of whatever this is.* Veronica leaves the package with a toss that represents her attitude toward these people and their stuff and heads back to her van. By the time she opens the van door, she can sense the idea coming in. *If your boss finds out about this, you'll be in deep trouble. These people in this house could complain. They could make a real stink. They could make this hard for you to get the raise you want.* Veronica drives away as the chatter continues, and she heads to deliver her next package. *I hate this job,* she thinks.

Veronica's critic has a belief that Veronica can't have the house, life, or job that she wants, a belief that is not serving her. She also has a complicated relationship with rules that make her rebel against them, but then she shames herself for violating them. She could benefit from loosening the hold that the critic has on her.

Day 3

INNATE WORTHINESS

Your work thus far has been to use your notebook to create new, positive ideas you are practicing. You've also done self-reflection to uncover reasons for holding on to the critic. I've highlighted the more common ones, including a belief that the critic is necessary to force you to do hard things. This one belief is so entrenched in our society that I am going to break it down for you, piece by piece.

We have a shared worship of hard work. This isn't a bad thing unless that shared worship takes the place of real love. We do that when we withhold love, or approval, of ourselves until we do hard things. We have created thought patterns that say, *I can't be trusted to do a hard thing unless I make myself do the hard thing.*

This truism gets played out in all sorts of ways. As we use brute force to make ourselves do things that we do not want to do, we erode our own trust in ourselves, which then leads to a greater dependency on the critic to motivate us. As we lose faith in our own ability to do the work, or the hard thing, that we think is required of us, we sink deeper into a relationship with the critic for our sense of motivation. When a person is struggling her way through her entire day, she eventually loses all faith in her own internal motivation, and eventually cedes all her power to the critic to push her through to completion.

We see this when people burn out and say, *I have no interest in life.* We see this when people fly off the handle and seem to rebel at even the tiniest additional responsibility. We see this when people lose their spark and sleepwalk through their days.

Sadly, many of these people think that the key to getting them out of this funk cycle is to take on a big challenge, overcome an obstacle, or force themselves to "put themselves out there." All of which are just more ideas, based in fear, of how to motivate you to do something you don't want to do.

The underpinning of all this is the idea that you, natural human that you are, are not to be trusted. That you, person who you are, can't accomplish anything unless you make yourself do it. That you, soul who you are, are flawed and need to prove yourself worthy. These are mistaken ideas to be healed.

To address this, we need to build up your belief in yourself, your goodness, your worthiness, and your enough-ness.

The critic tears you down and tricks you into thinking that you must prove yourself worthy. Worthiness, however, is never earned. It is innate. It is so innate that it can't be earned. It's there, waiting for you to claim it.

Our work, for today, is to claim our worthiness. You will practice saying *I am worthy* every day. You will create notes for yourself all around the house saying *I am worthy exactly as I am.* You will practice saying *I am worthy* throughout your day, until it becomes an idea you can live with.

A belief in your worthiness is not a "nice to have." It's an essential belief if you want to present to the world as a whole, healed person. It's a truth so fundamental that you forgot about it. It's a belief you will need to carry you through the process of losing the critic.

The fundamental underpinning of a critic is a belief in unworthiness. If you can cut down that underlying foundation, you have a chance of succeeding in leading a critic-less life.

Saying *I am worthy* is the first step. The second step, when confronted with life situations that challenge your worthiness, is to meet them with a retort: *I am worthy exactly as I am.*

Fortunately, life serves us exactly what we need to grow and expand, so you will find yourself in situations where you will initially feel unworthy. And that will be your cue to stand tall and proclaim, *I am worthy*, and all feelings of unworthiness will disappear.

Here is where you could, if you were listening to the critic, go into a downward spiral. You could, if the critic were in the lead, assume that life was telling you—through these situations—that you are unworthy. Not true. Life is helping you claim your worthiness for yourself.

You are the only person who can claim your worthiness. No one can gift it to you. No one can create the belief for you. No one can come in and say, *Now you are worthy of life*. You must do this work yourself, for yourself.

To begin, say *I am worthy*. Notice the life events that help you claim worthiness. Then, say *I am worthy* when you notice your critic. Here are examples.

If you take an afternoon off, and you have thoughts that say *I didn't accomplish anything today* (thoughts of the critic), then proclaim, *I am worthy of taking time for myself.*

If you put on an outfit that you don't enjoy, and the critic says, *You are too fat*, then speak back at that thought and say, *I am worthy exactly as I am.*

If you screw up at work or school, and the critic has the scene on perpetual rerun in your brain, stop and say, *Whatever happened today, I know myself as worthy.*

This is going to be the hardest part because a part of you believes the critic. You think the critic is pointing out the truth or what is obvious. Whatever belief you put in the critic, take a stand for putting a greater belief in yourself.

A worthiness practice is a lifelong endeavor that grows into a self-love practice that will sustain you for the rest of your days. And it starts today, as you have the opportunity to claim your worthiness without needing to prove yourself, produce anything, or do anything.

Worthiness is about existence. I like to say, *I am worthy, I exist, and I matter.* These three ideas are similar and supporting to me. They anchor me to my truth and help me express my worthiness to be. They also give a little color to worthiness, which can be an abstract concept.

Worthiness, to me, is a claim of today. It's a claim that who I am, where I am, and as I am are all things that are perfectly OK. I need not change, even though I could hold a desire to change. My worthiness never changes; only my awareness of it changes. It's a fundamental truth for every person, and it's a belief that will set you free.

When you are among people who make you feel small, claim your worthiness. When you feel inept or unskilled, claim your worthiness.

When you can't find the words to express the true you, fall back to this: *I am worthy no matter what*. Every situation in life is a chance to say, *I am worthy of being here*.

We all have reasons we feel unworthy, and those reasons are as unique as we are. If you want to delve into your reasons for feeling unworthy, journal to uncover your blocks. But don't stop practicing saying *I am worthy*. Ever.

Each time we encounter new situations, our fears come out to play. An excellent way through that fear is to claim your worthiness in that new situation. It can also be a comfort to start your day with a practice of saying *I am worthy*. Every day is a new opportunity to claim yourself as worthy of being alive.

Worthiness and aliveness go hand in hand. When you feel unworthy, you lose your spark. But when you regain a belief in your own worthiness—which you will if you practice—you regain your spark. You find a desire to take action, rather than forcing yourself to do something. You find projects that interest you, rather than doing only what you should. You find a deep inner connection to your soul that propels you into a life you love. And in that work, you lose connection to the critic.

The critic pumps out ideas of unworthiness all day. It tells you that you look too shabby to eat at that restaurant. It tells you that you need to work harder to gain acclaim at work. It tells you that you aren't good enough to live a life fueled by your wants and passions. It tells you that you are better off staying home and staying small.

Learning to recognize the critic is an essential skill in learning to dismantle the critic. My critic tells me that I can't, I shouldn't, and I better not. If you find yourself using any of those words, know that you are listening to the critic and not your authentic self. Below is a list of ideas anchored in fear, followed by ideas anchored to love. These may help you see the critic's ubiquitous role in your life.

Fear: I can't.
Love: Let's try.
Fear: I won't.
Love: Here is what I prefer.
Fear: Don't.
Love: Here is the option I want.
Fear: Get away from me.
Love: Honor my boundary.
Fear: I better not.
Love: I am interested but unsure how to proceed.
Fear: Don't talk to me.
Love: I prefer time alone right now.
Fear: There are no good solutions.
Love: There are always solutions coming in for me.

This is just a sampling of ways that fear is part of our shared lexicon. As you loosen the critic, you will speak the language of love. Those words are *I want, I am interested, I desire*, or *I prefer*. You will no longer react to what others are doing, and you will instead say, clearly and plainly, what you want. This is a skill that to practice another day, but for today, open yourself to the idea that fear might sound like something you did not see as fear.

Your critic is part of your life today. That's where you are. Our goal is to break up with that critic and experience life on our terms. Your work, for today, is to focus on worthiness and practicing, with

deliberate intent, the idea that you are worthy exactly as you are. If it helps, try out one of these statements:
- There is nothing wrong with me, and I am worthy.
- I have nothing to prove to anyone; I am worthy.
- I am intact, complete, and have a right to exist; I am worthy as I am.
- I need not seek approval from anyone, as I know myself as worthy.
- I have the right and the responsibility to claim myself as worthy. I am.
- My worthiness is innate, and I claim myself as worthy.

Try to find words that feel good to you. I went through a phase of saying *There is nothing wrong with me* for days until the truth of it sunk in and thus allowed me to claim my worthiness.

You aren't flawed, broken, or beyond repair. You are a human having an experience of life, and you are learning as you go. Exactly as you planned. Claim your worthiness as a sort of hedge, if you must, but claim it today.

If you need help with reminders, here are ideas:
- Put a Post-it next to your workspace saying *I am worthy*.
- Take a picture of that Post-it note, and make it your background on your phone.
- Set a reminder on your phone to recur every day, saying *I am worthy*. Let it keep appearing on your lock screen, and each time you see the reminder, affirm your worth.
- Send an email to yourself each day for the next thirty days, saying *I am worthy* in the subject line. Schedule it to send at a different time each day.

- Create a sign that you post on your mirror at home. Look yourself in the eye and claim your worthiness as you brush your teeth.
- Make a new rule that every time you go to the bathroom, you will say *I am worthy*.
- Ask a friend to text you on occasion to remind you to say *I am worthy*. Do the same for her.
- Tell your housemates that you are working on a belief in your worthiness, and then update them each day at dinner as to your new project. Lead by example, and your entire family will follow.
- Start each segment of your day with a statement of your worthiness. Before you leave for work. Before every meeting. Before each class. Before you commute. Before you eat. Before you go to bed. Anchor each segment in love and worthiness, and soon you'll believe that you too—just like everyone else—are worthy.

TAKEAWAYS

- You are worthy, and you are worthy of life without the critic.
- There are many ways to practice a new idea; go all in on reminders to help yourself.
- You can reach a stage where the critic goes silent, and it's worth the practice to get there.

Mike has big plans, big dreams, and a foolproof plan. He will work as hard as he must for any goal he sets. He never takes *no* for an answer. And he always seeks to out-effort, outdo, and outsell the competition. When his goals feel bigger than he can accomplish, he is happy. Mike regularly checks in with his own inner compass for guidance, but when the answer says, *Take a break*, he pushes through that small voice and instead mimics the role models in his life, pouring himself into work and finding value. Mike finds it hard to take a day off, and even vacations feel untenable to him. He just can't get the thrill of completing a sale in any other area of his life. He leans into that thrill and makes work his number-one passion.

Mike has a tenuous relationship with the critic, one that suggests that Mike's worth is tied to how many sales he makes. This connection could be a fun way to pass the time but also could become a tether, keeping Mike from finding joy in other places. Mike could work on reframing his relationship with the critic to see that his work can be fun but does not determine his worth or his joy.

Day 4

WORTHINESS APPLIED

With your new practice of a belief in your worthiness, let's explore what that means.

When you believe you are worthy, you no longer care what others think. Their opinions become points of interest but are not relevant to you.

When you believe you are worthy as you are, you no longer strive to succeed. Instead, you cruise to success doing what you love.

When you have a belief in your innate worthiness, you stand taller, stride more confidently, and enter every room with a sense of purpose: to be yourself.

Those who are worthy have no need to pretend. Those who know themselves as worthy have no reason to hold back their emotions. Those who practice their worthiness daily grow in power and in a belief in themselves.

Worthiness underpins every great success. When you believe you are worthy, you see the future as a series of choices, and you select the ones that most appeal to you. When you cultivate your belief in worthiness, you set yourself up for success every day.

Worthiness will affect every area of your life. Once you develop this belief, you will go through a period of impatience with any person or situation that seems to suggest you are not worthy. And you will rise to meet those people and situations with a total and complete belief that you are worthy of what you want and more.

Worthiness has no downside. There is no punishment for believing you are worthy. In fact, the only repercussion comes when you believe you aren't worthy and instead seek to rely on your critic to tell you your value.

That, in essence, is what the critic plays on: your value as a human being. It makes sure you think that your value is conditional and must be earned, and thereby blocks you from seeing that your value is intrinsic and cannot be taken away.

I believe we each have reasons to feel good about ourselves. We do good deeds. We overcome our fears. We tackle something that, at first, we didn't believe we could do. Those are all wonderful reasons to celebrate, to feel good, and to see yourself as good and worthy. But do not allow those actions to become conditions to your worthiness. Make your worthiness unconditional and set yourself free.

The ties that bind us are our own limiting beliefs of who we are and what we are capable of. Your critic is your jailer, to whom you gave the keys. Take back your power by staking a claim for unconditional worthiness, with these exercises:

- Take a day off work or away from your family. Make no plans and set no agenda. Move from moment to moment based on what feels good, and with each segment, affirm, *I am worthy of listening to myself.*

- Make a list of people you admire. Put yourself on the list and say, *I am worthy of my own admiration.*
- Take your notebook out and make a list of your goals. Say, for each goal, *I am worthy of achieving my goals.*
- Keep a running list of new experiences you would like to have in your life. Next to each, write *I am worthy of experiencing life on my terms.*
- Tell someone how you honestly feel and then tell yourself, *I am worthy of expressing all my emotions.*
- Create a chart of the number of times you downplay your strengths, defer a compliment, or say, *That was no big deal.* With each time you do this, say, *I am worthy of praise.*
- Mark off each day as it comes to a close, and say, *I am worthy of a good night's sleep tonight.*

Worthiness needs to become your default, so we are looking for ways to practice saying *I am worthy,* and then adding in something more specific to anchor it to your reality. Many of us need tangible examples before an idea becomes real to us, so I have provided a long list of examples so you can choose three that work for you. Start using them as soon as today.

- Put on a great outfit, and say, *I am worthy of great clothes every day.*
- Buy yourself jewelry or a watch, and say, *I am worthy of adorning myself with things I love.*
- Make a meal that suits your taste, and say, *I am worthy of cooking a meal for myself.*
- Go out for a walk, and repeat, *I am worthy of perfect health.*

- Take your dog for a walk, and say, *I am worthy of love and companionship.*
- Read the newspaper, and say, *I am worthy of choosing what I allow into my experience.*
- Get a haircut, and say, *I am worthy of caring for my appearance.*
- Tell someone to honor your boundaries, and say, *I am worthy of setting my own boundaries.*
- Do something just for fun, and say, *I am worthy of fun and frivolity.*
- Keep a diary of all that you loved about today, and write, *I am worthy of having great days.*
- Take a sip of water, and say, *I am worthy of fresh, clear water.*
- Keep a note on your phone that says *I am worthy of anything that I want today.*
- Tell your family you are no longer doing the dishes, and say, *I am worthy of speaking my mind.*
- Keep your ideas to yourself, and say, *I am worthy of choosing when I want to speak.*
- Start a new program to better your life, and say, *I am worthy of investing in me.*
- Kick off your shoes at the end of the day, and say, *I am worthy of relaxing tonight.*
- Make your bed, and say, *I am worthy of preparing this bed for me.*
- Take a friend out for coffee, and say, *I am worthy of having friends in my life.*
- Clean up your desk, and say, *I am worthy of a space that feels good to me.*

This isn't hard. The hardest part is to remember that you are now claiming worthiness until it becomes a habit. Here is what I suggest: choose a list that resonates with you. Where you know you have a little work to do in claiming your worthiness. Where you know that a claim of worthiness would be a new step for you. Where you sense that you have the potential to grow if you believe that you are worthy.

Make your list and write it in your notebook. Here is the formula: *When I [insert action], I will claim my worthiness.* This alone will be a process of claiming your worthiness. Then use your tools and best ideas to help you set reminders to claim your worthiness and bring it down to the specific thing or feeling that you are worthy of.

We all have hang-ups about what we think we can experience. Only you know yours. If you want to select from the above examples, choose the ones that seem the most far-fetched to you. Choose the ones that seem like a stretch for you. Choose the ones that grab your attention because you had not thought about your worthiness in this area before.

Here is why this works: it's you practicing a new belief and then making it real. We all change our thinking over time, but I have found that it changes the easiest when I can tie my new belief into the life I am living. Then it is no longer an abstract concept but becomes an idea that is tethered to your life, today.

Worthiness is the topic of the day, and your commitment to this will pay dividends, not only in losing your critic but also in bolstering your confidence and belief of what you expect from life. When I do this work, I always find new things I can attach my worthiness to. I find new ideas where I did not realize I was limiting or judging myself. I find new tidbits about myself, which keeps life interesting.

As you do this work, you'll notice subtle shifts in your posture, in your outlook, and in your expectations. That's a great thing. Get used to the idea of expecting more from life, as that is an idea the critic will try to quash. But you aren't going to allow the critic to do that.

Instead, you will do the work and anchor your worthiness to everything you can think of today. You'll do the same tomorrow, and keep going, until your worthiness game becomes your default. You'll walk into a room one day and say, *I am worthy of a seat at the table.* And you will know that you—the true you—has arrived.

I have found that my inner essence, my soul, has no hang-ups around worthiness. She knows herself as worthy everywhere she goes. You are now learning to do the same.

TAKEAWAYS

- Worthiness is your birthright. No one can take it away from you, but you could decide not to claim it.
- Claim your worthiness in all areas of your life; watch your confidence and your spirit grow.
- Worthiness is yours and yours alone; you take nothing from another by claiming your worthiness.
- Those who claim their worthiness light the way for others.

Kathy sets the table for dinner and looks at the clock. She sighs because no one is home yet, and the food is ready and on the stove. *Where are they?* she mumbles to herself. She knows what will happen. Jenny will walk through the door, offering excuses around traffic and being stuck late on a call at work. Jeremy will come in and say that basketball ran late. And Penny will walk through the door, eager to see her mother and ready to eat. *At least one person appreciates me,* Kathy muses. She tends to the food on the stove, doing her best to keep it from drying out. She checks her phone, paces around the house, and finally, in a fit of anger, texts them to see where they are: *Anyone coming home for dinner tonight? Would be nice to know.* She drops the phone in a huff and then checks the food again. *No one would do this for me,* she thinks.

Kathy's critic seems to think that Kathy's highest, best use is tending to the needs of others while repressing her own needs and wants. This mistaken critic could be dealt with if Kathy was willing to step into the lead of her own life and cast herself as the star of the production that is her life. Kathy could also benefit from learning to identify and articulate what she wants, rather than hopelessly trying to anticipate the needs of others.

Day 5

HEAL YOUR PAST

Your work for this project of losing your critic is all inner work. Those words used to scare me because I was accustomed to the critic telling me what was wrong with me. I equated inner work with a direct interaction with the critic where I was told, in no uncertain terms, what I needed to fix. Instead of going down that path, I wisely avoided doing inner work.

I want to set the table for you as to what inner work really is: it's a process where you love every part of yourself. That's it. You go back into your own past, see yourself clearly, and still say, *I love myself.* You think about who you are and what you want, and then you say, *I still love myself.* You reflect on your own present experience, and you say, *I love myself exactly as I am today.*

This isn't hard or even a problem to overcome. It's an opportunity to call yourself home. See inner work this way: you are collecting every version of yourself so you can fortify yourself for the life ahead. Not because life is hard, but because you want to feel whole every day for the rest of your life.

Wholeness occurs when you love up all your pieces, and then they come home. Wholeness benefits you because you feel grounded, centered, and clear. Wholeness is easy once you know the process to get there.

If you have a strong critic, as I once did, you will avoid revisiting any past incident when you feel you fell short. That's smart, as the critic will try to tear you apart. But eventually, you need to pick up your pieces, and I want you to see yourself as the fiercest, most loving protector of every version of you.

It's you versus the critic, and you will win. You can stand up for yourself, your prior selves, and your wants, and tell the critic that it has it wrong.

You'll revisit the past. You will be reminded of an incident in childhood when you were reprimanded or did something you thought was bad. And in that moment, you will stop and say, *I love who I was on that day.* You aren't going to justify your conduct. You aren't going to judge your conduct. You will love and simply hold yourself in love until you feel a sense of peace wash over you.

As you do this work, I have found it useful to set intentions. Pull out your notebook and write these down:

I intend to love every version of me, no matter what he did, said, or thought.

I intend to love myself so completely that every part of me feels welcome to come home.

I intend to do this work naturally, easily, and as I go about my day.

With those intentions, it's time to allow your mind to bring you memories from the past. You'll remember a time you cheated, badmouthed, or stole. And you will love yourself. You'll remember a time you failed, fell down, or hated another. And you will love yourself. You'll be reminded of a time when you hated yourself, heaped criticism on yourself, and made yourself small, and still, you will say that you love that prior version of you. That's right: you will love yourself for having a critic.

There is a fine line between blame and responsibility. I want you to see yourself on the side of power. Meaning, if you take responsibility for the critic, then you have power over the critic. So this is not about blame, and I encourage you to steer clear of blame, guilt, and shame. Instead, step into your power and say, *I created this critic for a good reason. And I love the version of me who created the critic.*

If you want to do this work in a more deliberate way, take out a blank sheet of paper, not in your notebook. On that paper, write out every transgression you can remember. The time you hit your sister. The time you blew up at your parents and caused them stress. The time you called in sick when you weren't. Write out your list of everything you think you did wrong.

With each transgression on that page, I want you to say, *I love the person who committed this act. I love who I was back then. I love how I acted.* Get to a place where you aggressively and consistently stand up for your prior selves.

Then, if you want to empower yourself even further, turn to your notebook and write out the opposite of the transgression. If you hit your sister, write *I am a good and loving sister*. If you gave your parents grief, write *I am a good and loving son*. If you quit a sports team out of spite, say *I am a great team player*. Take your transgression list and turn it into the messages that you need to hear to heal.

I believe that each of us has within us the power to heal ourselves. And this is the path that I have found that works. Take the ideas that you are carrying even today about your past and use those ideas to create custom messages that will soothe your wounds. If you resist these messages, then you need to hear them more. See your resistance as a sign that you, personally, would experience a great benefit if you gave yourself healing messages.

Our responsibility is to heal our own wounds so we can present to the world as a healed and whole person. Do your part by tending to your own wounds.

The critic may come out to play and tell you that you suck, are worthless, or are bad. Gently say, *That's not true.* And then say, *I love myself even though I am still criticizing myself.*

Here is where you might have developed a habit of tuning out the critic because the words were so painful that you repressed and stopped allowing them to be heard. But your body felt them every time your mind went into critical mode. You might need to slow down and ask yourself, *What is it about this past event that gives me distress or unease?* Let the critic have her say and pour out all her criticisms. When the diatribe is over, say, *And still, I love myself.*

See the critic as an overinflated balloon. Filled with fear. When you allow those fears to come forward, you heal them. When you allow those fears to be heard, the balloon deflates. And then it's up to you to stand in a position of love and say, *And still, I am choosing to side with love.*

A critic is an idea based in fear. When you are a soul created in love. Fear doesn't stand a chance around you when you are in your authentic, loving state. Fear is a nonissue once you grow in love. Take a stand for yourself, choose to be on the side of love, and knock that critic off its perch each time you love yourself even when you did something you judge as bad.

Here is where your belief in reconciliation will help you. What we are reconciling is you with you. How and whether you reconcile with another person is a separate process and has nothing to do with your ability to reconcile with yourself. In fact, I have found that once I reconcile with myself, I easily find reconciliation with another person. Stated differently, once I love the person I was when I took the action I now regret, I more easily find a way to love the person I was entangled with when I took the action.

Your past is over and has a hold on you only to the extent that you haven't loved the prior version of you who took the actions you regret. Free yourself from your past by loving who you were, even as you hold a desire to behave differently in the future. We all have actions we regret or feel badly about. Those of us with a critic have these daily, so you will gain the most from loving up your past.

Here is why this works: you are bravely using your own spirit to help you find love again. What better use for your spirit than that? It seems logical to me that unconditional love would want to love things up. You are simply opening the door by opening your mind to love.

As you do this work, you'll feel more at peace with the past. When a tense or difficult blast from the past appears, make time to sit with the event and simply say, *And still I love myself.* Over and over. Until the love seems to take over and do the work for you.

When I do this work, I find it to be iterative. When a painful memory surfaces, I love it. And then the next time it comes up, I love it more. Eventually it seems to dissipate from my experience, each time conjuring up weaker and weaker emotions. Until I reach a point where I can recall the past event and not flinch. I can sit with the past event with compassion and clarity and see the past neutrally. That's when true healing occurs because you detect your own past patterns of thought that caused you to act.

The critic, as I said, is the biggest block you have keeping you from inner work. You fear the deluge of negative judgments that the critic will pile on you. Let those criticisms all come forward, and then hold a space of love to heal them all up.

Once you become adept at this—and you will with even a little practice—you'll soon get excited to call home your missing pieces. The pieces of you who carried the shame. The pieces of you who wallowed in the guilt. The pieces of you who had crazy ideas about what she did wrong.

We all have a list of transgressions that, if someone else read it, they would say, *You're nuts*. Meaning, those actions are no big deal. Using your role as a dispassionate observer, see if you can reach a place of seeing your past not as a problem but as a life well lived. You are not a saint, a monk, or even a person who came into life to live a perfect life. You are a soul who came to experience joy. You just didn't know how to do that when you were told to "be good," "keep quiet," and "take care of others." We'll tackle these ideas another day. For today, your work is complete, unconditional love to every version of you that has ever existed.

TAKEAWAYS

- Inner work is loving up your past selves and accepting yourself as you are, and as you were.
- Loving yourself is easy once you drop the critic.
- Each version of you holds power, so you want to call all your pieces home with love.

Cameron shakes the last cigarette from the pack, lights it, and thinks, *I need to stop doing this. This is so bad for me.* He takes a long inhale, relaxes, and looks around his apartment. He sees that clothes are strewn everywhere and makes a mental note to clean up. He sees the overfull ashtray and thinks, *I live like such a slob.* He looks down at his protruding belly, rubs it, and thinks, *I should not have had pizza for dinner.* As he finishes his cigarette, he stands up and picks up the clothing, only to think, *This is such a waste of time. This place is a mess that it's not worth cleaning up for myself. I'm going to bed.*

Cameron's critic has taken over his life. He would do well to immerse himself in a project of releasing the critic, finding the loving voice of his inner wisdom, and starting over from there, one day at a time. He could also benefit from therapy or counseling to help him see the thought patterns that are dangerous for his health.

Day 6

UNCONDITIONAL LOVE

The critic isn't bad. It's just mistaken. It thinks you need to be kept safe, which means that it tells you what went wrong so you can fix it. The critic has this crazy, twisted idea that if you perfect yourself, then you will be accepted. If you cure all your defects, then you'll be deemed good. If you right all your wrongs, then you'll be welcomed into society as someone who is worthy. If you fix your mistakes, then you'll be permitted to love yourself.

But what the critic misses is this fundamental idea: you are unconditionally loved as you are. You can't earn that. You can't pay for that. You can't even get away from that. It just is.

This is where thoughtful, rational thinking can help you loosen the hold of the critic.

Unconditional love, by definition, has no conditions. There is no barrier to entry and certainly no fine print to read. It's unconditional. It's also free, which makes it a rare bird in our society. We are all so jaded that most of us look askance at anything and anyone who gives away something for free. We assume it has no value, and we assume that we are better off paying for what we want.

But if you can sit with the idea of unconditional love and let the idea of a one-way flow of love sink in, you'll see that your critic's wacky if-then statements are simply untrue. There can't be an if-then when the love is free. There can't be anything to earn, because you already have it. There can't be anything to fix, because you're not broken. You are simply working your way into a knowing of unconditional love.

That's how I see my mistakes. I forgot who I was. I forgot that I'm allowed to express myself and do what I want. I forgot that the only rules I truly believe in are the rules that tell me to love myself and others. I forgot that I am worthy and don't need to prove myself.

The idea of unconditional love isn't new and isn't that controversial among the spiritually curious. Yet we all seem to fall asleep and forget that we aren't required to do anything to be loved. Nothing. There are no conditions to entry. In fact, we can't *not* access it, as it's keeping us all alive. The best course of action is to accept it.

Accept that you are unconditionally loved.

To do this, you sit with the idea of unconditional love, and you welcome it in. When I go into a deep meditation, I can feel that love; it's that powerful. But it also is something I seem to know on a level I can't explain. I simply know myself as loved.

For those of us with a critic, we might not believe in unconditional love. That's OK. Because you can create that belief and then step into the flow. With practice.

As we did with earlier sections, we will choose a set of words that work for us. Even if you don't believe, you will benefit from this exercise. In fact, you might benefit the most, as you don't have preconceived notions around what it means to be unconditionally loved. Choose from one of the options below to add to your daily practice:

- I am unconditionally loved.
- I am loved completely and wholly, with no conditions whatsoever on that love.
- I am a recipient of unconditional love and support.
- I am open to seeing myself as unconditionally loved.
- I am ready to embrace the benefits of being unconditionally loved.

That last one works for me. When I can see the benefits of practicing the idea that I am loved, I am more motivated to practice. And the benefits are huge.

When you believe yourself to be unconditionally loved, the only person you try to impress is yourself. That's the only opinion you care about. You accept the love coming to you, accept that you don't need to earn it, and then go about life working toward your own good opinion of yourself. You work harder on issues and people who mean a lot to you, as you are working toward passing on the love you have received. It's an endless loop you couldn't get out of if you tried.

When you build up a belief in unconditional love, your silly if-then ideas just fall away. I don't prove myself worthy of love. I have it. I don't earn love. It's there, regardless of what I do. And I don't worry about taking too much love, because there is an infinite supply.

Our rational minds, once put to work on this idea, eventually find a way to grasp that this flow is coming whether we accept it or not.

So why not accept it and run with it?

I embraced unconditional love because I was tired of resisting it. I had created so many barriers that I was a virtual brick wall of ideas, all saying, *I will prove myself worthy of being loved*. It was exhausting. Once I gave up that wall-building, all my defenses came down. Including my critic. What needed time to catch up were my old patterns of thought that went to critical ideas as a default setting.

The path for each is unique, so I won't presuppose that your path will look like my path. But here is what I experienced once I built up the idea that I was unconditionally loved.

I stopped caring what anyone thought of me. I woke up each day with eager anticipation for the day and what it would bring me. I became curious about my thought patterns and saw them as something that could change. I started writing, expressing myself, and showing up as my authentic self. I began to experience more joy, more laughter, and more fun in my life. I embraced my mistakes and even saw them as benefiting me. I began to look forward to each day as a way of learning more about myself. I stopped complaining and started celebrating. I grew in confidence and clarity. I knew instantly what was for me and what was not. I had good ideas all the time. And, most importantly, I lost the critic.

I can't pinpoint the day, but at some point, I realized that I was no longer being hard on myself. I was being nice to myself. I was no longer trying to motivate myself with fear, and instead, I was doing only what I wanted. I was no longer listening to the critic; I was listening to my authentic self.

For those who live life like this, you have my awe. I truly had no idea how awesome it is not to have that chatter in my brain all the time. I had no idea that the critic was a problem. I had no idea that the critic was the single biggest thing standing between me and my soul.

Many of us with loud critics, and a background in traditional religions, have a belief that the critic is our soul. That our souls are the ones telling us all the ways we are defective, wrong, and in need of repair. That our souls are the ones harping on us to do more, achieve more, and keep others happy. That our souls are the part of us responsible for making us feel so lousy all the time.

This one idea was such a block to me that I am passionate about getting the word out. In case you didn't know, souls deal in love. Souls speak words of love. Souls do pretty much nothing but love. As best I can tell, souls are synonymous with love.

When you are thinking, *Why did I screw up?* That's your ego. When you are saying, *I am such a mess*, that's your critical ego. When you are simmering in a state of fear, you are fully in tune with the ego and are not listening to your own soul.

This one idea set me free from the critic in ways I am still reeling over. All those harsh retorts? Not my soul. All that guilt, shame, and blame? Not my soul. All that second-guessing and circling in uncertainty? Not my soul. In fact, my soul was the one who helped me to see that the critic had a purpose.

The critic's purpose, as I said, is to keep you safe. It simply equates safety with conformity. The critic can't appreciate that safety is a result of living aligned with your spirit, not tuning it out. The critic can't see that life with your spirit is better than a life without it.

I now make it a regular practice to call in my spirit to help me. This practice seems to retrain my mind to see the benefits of the spirit-led life. It also helps me get comfortable with the idea that a spirit-led life is not what I thought it would be.

Again, here is where the critic did me a disservice. I thought a spirit-led life was one where you always did what you did not want, to curry favor with the powers that be. I thought a spirit-led life was boring, depressing, and filled with people I didn't prefer. I thought the spirit-led life was one of constant self-criticism and betterment for the greater good.

What a crock.

Now that I am on the other side of that limited and fearful thinking, I can see why I—and many others—run from spirituality. We think we will run into the critic if we step into the flow of love. It's just the opposite. You step into your birthright—access to the flow of unconditional love—and you lose your desire to self-criticize.

Your work, for today, is to add to your practice an idea around the availability of unconditional love. Don't get hung up on who is doing the loving. Just know that you are loved. As that belief grows in your experience, you will notice feelings of love in your heart, in your body, and in your energy field.

TAKEAWAYS

- Unconditional love is free and has no conditions to access it.
- Your critic doesn't understand unconditional love, so it runs away.
- Your best move is to allow this free, universal resource to guide you in life.

Marguerite plays the cello in the school orchestra, and she is eyeing the first chair. She can see herself in that seat, being the one called out as the best cellist in the orchestra. As she thinks of that goal, she remembers that Andy also wants that seat and that he has so many more supporters than she does. It seems like every teacher loves him and that he basks in knowing he can charm anyone into giving him what he wants. In fact, Andy is so smug that Marguerite makes it a point to avoid him. She only watches him from afar and sees how he gets what he wants in life while she clearly is the better musician. She can't seem to shake the idea that he is the one standing between her and her goals.

Marguerite could see that her projections onto Andy are her own critic helping her to see a want that she doesn't believe she can have. She could work on losing her critic, owning her dreams, and find relief.

Day 7

GO EASY

As you notice the critic in your life, you will become increasingly impatient. You'll say, *Why did my mind have to go there?* Or *Why do I keep circling on this negative event?* Or *What good is it to try to lose my critic when there is so much about me I don't like?*

These are all natural progressions as you notice the extent of your critic. I want to prepare you for this stage, as it can be frustrating. You feel like you are ready to be done; you are doing the work of building up new ideas, but you are still experiencing old thought patterns of the critical mind. Here is where you could need a break, to let the body catch up to the mind.

As I did the work of surrendering my critic, I found that I would have the urge to walk, to shake, or to stretch. My body seemed to want to release energy. My body seemed to say, *There are deep pockets of old thinking being held here*, and *Let's stretch and get that out of here*. I would find myself in a downward dog pose, or in a deep hip stretch on the floor, and the feeling of release was amazing.

For today, your work is to tune in to your body to see if you have any area that feels like it needs a release. Do you want to stretch, yawn, or move around? Do you want to adjust your position or scratch your head? Do you find yourself walking around the house, not sure why you are in a room? I see these as signs that the body wants to move and release energy. Which makes good sense to me. Our bodies store all sorts of memories, and the critic is just an old idea that you are getting rid of for good.

If you hit this stage, here is what to notice:

- You may feel fidgety. You might get up often, change position, or simply walk to another room. Honor your body's desire to move, and say, *I am letting go of the critic. This is fun.*
- You might sleep more. I found that some nights, I slept ten to twelve hours. It was a sign that my body and my spirit were processing old stuff, and I saw sleep as an excellent tool to help me process smoothly.
- You may, on the other hand, have nights where you don't sleep. You'll feel wide-awake. You'll feel like your energy wants to move. Again, honor the energy and let it do its work.
- You might find yourself rubbing your body, shaking your body, or wanting to aggressively move your body. Let this be a sign that you are making good progress, and say, *I am so glad this stuck energy* is moving out.
- You could experience a spike in hunger, wanting to eat, or eating foods that seem comforting to you. Go with it and say, *I am undoing years of critical self-talk, and I will not self-criticize for what I eat. I lovingly accept all my cravings as benefiting me.*

- You could experience a desire to be alone, to be in nature, or to sequester yourself in your room. I see this as time spent realigning with your true self. Which is always a good move. Welcome it in.
- You might seek out soothing self-care routines as a way of relief and pleasure. Long baths or showers. Spa appointments. Lovingly putting on lotion or prepping yourself for the day. Lean into these routines as you dispel the critical mind that saw these practices as a waste of time. Prolong them, savor them. And as you do, say, *I am doing this for me, and I am worth it.*
- You could find yourself at odds with your present experience as you associate your current situation with the critic. For this, you will need to either break free or set an intent to free yourself of the critic while you stay in place. My personal suggestion? Stay in place and do the work of breaking up with the critic now, as you'll only have to do it later if you try to move to a new situation. This is the time for self-love and acceptance, not new ideas and big plans.
- Your own mind may play tricks on you. It will drag you into a thought pattern that you know is unhelpful, negative, and judgmental. Be patient. Notice the thought pattern, then gently say, *I can choose to give my attention to something else.* Then change the subject.

The process of losing the critic is a *process*. That means that you'll cycle through breakthroughs and setbacks. You'll take two steps ahead and one step back. You'll be soaring one day, then feel the backlash the next.

That's OK. That's normal. That's how we all learn.

Iterative learning has you repeat a lesson, over and over, until it sticks. That's all we are doing. Gentle, effective iterative learning that is moving you from a person who self-criticizes by default to a person who self-celebrates by default. We are a long way from a habit of self-celebration, so don't worry about that today. Just know that we are undoing old programming and then welcoming in new programming. One day at a time.

My advice is that you rest, take a break, and prepare yourself to see the signs of the changes you are about to experience. A good use of this day is to journal in your notebook about the things you look forward to once you lose the idea that the critic is beneficial to your life. Here are ideas to get you started:

- When you lose a critic, you gain your spirit. You'll feel more energetic, more positive, and full of better ideas.
- When the critic pattern leaves, you have the opportunity to create a new pattern of thinking that says, *This life is awesome, I am doing great, and life only gets better and better.* These are fun, uplifting ideas that help you succeed.
- As the critic dissipates, you lose a taste for criticizing others. This frees up energy you can use for your personal projects and goals.
- When you no longer self-criticize, you grow in confidence, clarity, and compassion.
- As you drop the habit of self-criticism, you gain new insights, have breakthrough ideas, and feel inspired every day.
- When you fully drop the habit, you feel a sense of calm, peace, and certainty as to the next steps in your life. You feel like

you are creating your future and not merely accepting it as it comes.
- You resee the past and love up all your prior selves. Each one feels like a homecoming.
- You reach alignment with your true self and realize that this is how you were meant to live.

Your work today is to take care of you. Be nice to you. Be gentle toward yourself. If you are a hard-charging, take-no-breaks kind of person, then you might struggle here. Just be ready to say, *I am listening to my body, myself, and my spirit. I will not be ruled by a fearful mind.*

TAKEAWAYS

- Personal transformation can stir up feelings and ideas; go easy on yourself.
- Look for self-care practices that you enjoy regardless of what anyone else thinks.
- Self-soothing self-talk is highly beneficial to you.

Natalie cannot believe her good luck. She scored two tickets to the concert that everyone wants to attend. She set her alarm and got up early to get in line, and now she is proudly holding the tickets in her hands. By midmorning, however, she realizes that the tickets are worth more if she sells them. Despite promising her daughter that they would attend the concert together, Natalie is now on ticket-reseller sites, seeing how much she can get for the tickets. She sees that she can quadruple her money with the sale and gladly offers up the tickets to the first buyer who agrees to her price. Natalie feels self-satisfied because she has turned a small amount of money into a small fortune, all in one day. But then her stomach drops when she realizes that she must tell her daughter what she has done. Embarrassed by her frugal ways, Natalie decides that the better course is to lie and tell her daughter that she didn't get the tickets and that the whole process is rigged against people like them. Natalie drives home and practices, over and over, the excuse she will tell her daughter, working herself into a place of true indignation at the world for denying them the tickets they want.

Natalie has an inner being who is trying to break free. Natalie could confront the critic who tells her she can't come clean with her own daughter and own up to her own thought patterns. Natalie could also benefit from being honest with herself as to her inner desire to grow her money. In general, Natalie's awareness of her thinking could help her break free of the critic for good.

Day 8

MICRO-MEDITATIONS

Yesterday, we took a break, and we set an intention to look for ways that our bodies might be telling us to slow down. I hope you heeded that advice. I hope you use a self-care practice that includes slowing down, listening to your body, and allowing yourself to integrate the new ideas with ease. This new habit will serve you for the rest of your life.

Easing your way through the process of losing your critic is the best route I have found. You can't muscle your way through. You allow your way through. And that allowance can take lots of different forms.

One of the easiest ways to allow is to meditate with an intention to ease your connection with the critic. That's how I see it. You have tuned yourself to a thought form that pumps out ideas of what is wrong. And you are ready to attach to a new idea that celebrates what is right and good about life.

To do this, sit in a quiet place, get comfortable, and focus on your breath. I am not sure why, but I have found that it's important to keep the focus of your inner intent on you. Meaning, down into your body.

Many of us spend more time up in our heads, and the key to losing that critic connection, for me, was spending time with my awareness down in my body. Not all day, but a few minutes when I could.

I would imagine myself inside a tiny elevator inside me, going down into my core. Just riding down slowly and going within. This got me out of my head and allowed me to keep the focus of my meditation on me. It gave me focus so I didn't get wrapped up in random thoughts. And it helped me regulate my breathing, as I was focused on my inside.

You don't need to meditate for long to feel the effects of this inner focus. In fact, I found great success in doing this for only a minute or two, throughout my day. When I sensed that I was going unaware (caught up in a story, worrying, or spooling out with my thinking), I would turn my attention to my inner world and breathe through it. And in that turning inward, I disconnected from the story that my mind was running.

The mind loves stories, and stories are a great way to experience life. Every memory we have is a story of what happened, from our perspective. Every dream we hold is a story of what we want to experience in the future. Every judgment we hold is a story of what we think should have happened based on the rules we are running in our mind.

Meditation allows those stories to calm down. Meditation allows those stories to dissipate so you can exercise your free will to choose a better story. Meditation creates space for you to disconnect from a story that is not serving you so you can connect to a story that is serving you.

The critic is a storyteller. It makes up rules, scenarios, and problems, and lets you know that you are the one who is common to all of them. The critic will spin out with a story, telling you all the things that could go wrong. The critic will prolong a story by telling you how you have been wronged. The critic will make up stories to keep you from straying too far from what is accepted, conformist, or the norm.

The key thing to recognize is that all of life is a story. No matter how factual you think you are, your perspective is always laced with you. Your beliefs. Your fears. Your wants. And your expectations.

In meditation, you disconnect from the stories. You let them all go so that you can, once you are done with meditation, create a story that better serves you and the life you want to live.

Better stories aren't lying. They are adjusting your talk track to set yourself up for success. They are you entering into a loving relationship with yourself so you can heal up your past. These stories allow you to use your own mind to find peace.

But before we get to the part where we create new stories, we must lose our connection to our existing stories. And meditation helps with that.

I used to dread meditation because I listened to the critic who said I was terrible at meditating. I listened to the critic who harped on me when my mind wandered in meditation. I listened to the critic say, *This is boring and stupid*. So let me disabuse you of any of your concerns over your ability to meditate.

Meditation can be as short as one minute and be effective. You aren't looking for a marathon session. You are looking for one minute of going within and breathing, with an intent that says, *I am ready to surrender my critic*.

During meditation, your mind will wander. No big deal. When you notice that your mind has wandered, come back to your center, in your core, and say, *I am home again. Hooray!*

Meditation can be hard if you have a loud critic. Hang in there and say, *I am doing this to lose the critic. I am doing this for one minute, and then I will stop. I am doing this for me.*

What this does, for me, is to create new patterns of thought that go within, rather than staying up in my head where the critic lives. Remember, the critic is just an idea. It's a complex idea, but it's nothing more than an idea. And you can disconnect from an idea if you choose to.

We all change our minds all the time. We often do it so easily we don't realize it. We decide that we don't want something we used to want. We decide that we are no longer interested in a project that once interested us. We decide that we are ready to move on from a situation we once found acceptable. We move between ideas all the time.

The practice of going within need not be reserved for when you are alone and quiet. You can do this as you eat. You can do this as you drive. You can do this as you wait in line. You can do this at a meeting. You can do this in class. You can do it all day, and each moment you go within feels like a tiny reclamation of your power.

I like visuals. And the visual that the critic is outside me, and that the true me is inside me, helps me to disconnect from the critic and lean into my own inner guidance. A moment of inner work is a moment when I stake a claim for the true me.

I now do this often throughout my day. I take a breath, I center myself, and I sink into me. With each return, I see myself as victorious. Winning. Being me. I see it as a tiny act of rebellion against the fear that pervades our society. I can now do this on autopilot, so I don't need to focus on it with my conscious mind. Yes, still I make it a point, when I recall, to go within.

Inside, I am safe. Inside, I am loved. Inside, I am better able to gather all my resources, then go back into life and conquer my goals.

A practice of micro-meditations can change you from a person who hates meditations to a person who welcomes in a moment of respite, on the inside. A series of micro-meditations can interrupt your fear patterns and cause you to accelerate your divorce with the critic. A habit of micro-meditations can become the habit of a lifetime, always bringing you back to center.

There is a time and place for longer meditations. I do them when I have downtime and can give them my attention. But when you are new to meditation, the thought of a long meditation alone can be daunting. Circumvent that fear by chopping up the meditation into moments of pause, and work up your confidence from there.

It helps if you give yourself great praise for even the smallest moment of a pause and a dip within. I say, *Good job, you*. I make it a point to do the same any time my mind wanders, and then I come back. It's the homecoming to celebrate, not the stray.

Your critic is noisy. As you lean into a practice of meditation, your mind will become quieter and quieter, which gives you a better chance of meeting the critic when it arrives. Because it will come back, over and over, until you develop new thought patterns that build you up rather than take you down. We'll get to building on another day, but you can start saying nice things to yourself today. You can start today saying, *I can meditate for one minute*. You can start today with an intention to quiet your mind as you meditate to loosen the grip fear has on you.

A practice of micro-meditations is today's work. Simply stop, breathe, and then dip inside your core. Stay there, breathing, until your mind wanders. Say, *That's OK*, and bring your attention back.

Your mind will wander again. That's OK; the homecoming is sweet. Return to your core and continue to breathe. You could wander 1,000 times in one meditation, and all that matters is that you come home 1,001 times.

Set a timer for a minute and breathe. Get into bed and breathe. Take a shower and breathe. Sit in traffic and breathe. Listen as others talk and breathe, keeping your focus inside you.

Another word for meditation is awareness, and if that word helps you, use it. Say, *I am going to spend one minute being aware of what's going on inside me.* Or *I am going to use my awareness to focus on me for one minute.* Or *I am aware, and I am choosing to quiet my mind.* See what words feel good to you, but continue with a practice of going within.

I like the words *safe*, *home*, and *inside*. They all conjure up ideas of cozy to me, and that's what I want to feel when I retreat within. There I am safe. There my fear disappears. There I am home again, right where I belong.

TAKEAWAYS

- Going within is one way to get out of the critical patterns in your head. Visualize yourself going into your core.
- Start with a habit of one-minute meditations. Just breathe into your core and let yourself be.
- Putting the awareness inside you always yields good results, so make it a practice all day to go within even when you aren't sure what you are looking for.

Ginger is about to board a flight to Europe when her phone pings. It's her mother, and it's not good news. It never is. Ginger looks at the text and decides that she should get out of line and call her mother, as she is frail and elderly. Ginger does so, only to find that her mother has lost her earrings and wants help finding them. Infuriated, Ginger hangs up and lines up to board the plane again. Her mind gets the better of her, however, and says, *She is your mom, and you have to be nice to her*. Ginger takes out her phone and calls back, only to find that her mother won't pick up the phone. Ginger sighs and boards the plane. The entire flight, she plays out what happened with her mom, and hops from righteous indignation to flaming anger to contrite daughter. She is not sure what the right thing to think is, so she orders her third drink and finally relaxes into her seat to turn off her mind from running scenarios.

Ginger's critic has rigid rules around how to interact with your parents, and how to do what is expected of you. Ginger's efforts to justify her behavior is her coping mechanism to give herself relief. She could benefit from taking a stand for her own well-being, first and foremost, and refusing to listen to the rules that the critic tries to place on her.

Day 9

MIRROR WORK

We've been together for over a week, and you are filling your notebook with kind and loving ideas. With strong and uplifting ideas. With words you need to heal. Today, we make it a point to practice those new ideas in front of a mirror.

Mirror work is something I resisted for a long time. That's because I had a pattern of thought that criticized myself when I looked in the mirror. I would look away within moments as a way of lessening the pain and tension of the critic. If you have trouble looking yourself in the eye in the mirror, then know that the critic is running in the background, affecting your behavior. And as I said in a prior section, we are not letting the critic win.

Find a safe space and bring a mirror. If you must do this in the bathroom with the door locked, do that. If you must go sit in your car, do that. If you must find a public space where you can be alone, go find one. This is that important. Your eyes are literally the windows to your soul, and you need your soul to overcome the critic.

When we practice new ideas in front of a mirror, we create powerful feedback loops that associate us with the new idea. The new idea becomes more tangible in our lives. The new idea becomes part of us in a way that defies understanding. The new idea seeps into our consciousness and takes hold.

On my own journey, I had an intuitive knowledge that mirror work was helpful, and I still resisted it. I am sharing my own experience here to help you get on board. Once I began, in earnest, to look myself in the eye and say nice things to myself, I experienced extreme movement forward in my personal journey. I began to write, express myself, and walk around in a near-constant state of happiness. I was more confident, more knowing, and more in love with everyone in my life. I was on fire at work, with my home projects, and with my own self-talk. It was a superpower I didn't see coming. And it started with mirror work.

To do mirror work, I stand in front of my bathroom mirror and look at myself. When my eyes want to drift away, I slowly bring them back. I stare into my own eyes. I hold an intent to love myself. I sit with my visual and let whatever comes forward come forward. Then, I pull out my lists of new ideas, and I practice.

I tell myself I can lose the critic. I tell myself I am worthy, enough, and free. I tell myself I am loved unconditionally and that I am doing this mirror work for me.

I read out the messages I need to hear. I read off the new ideas I know will help me break free of the critic. I read, to myself, all the ideas that I am holding in my notebook.

At the end, I take a deep breath. I look myself in the eye. And then I thank myself for showing up to reclaim my power.

That's what mirror work is to me: the greatest power reclamation I have ever experienced. It's as if I took all the power I gave to the critic and gave it, instead, to myself. For my purposes. For my projects. For my goals.

When you look in the mirror, focus on your pupils. Look deeply into your eyes. This keeps you from judging your appearance or noticing what you are wearing. It allows you to deeply connect and see that there is a soul in there, waiting to emerge. There is a spirit in you that cannot be denied. There is more to you than meets the eye.

Mirror work is so powerful that I resisted it when I felt I wasn't ready for positive change in my life. Which was simply my critic keeping me small. There is never a wrong time for positive change in your life. There is never a bad time for saying nice things to yourself. There is never a problem with wanting more from life.

That is, in essence, why you are reading this book. On an intuitive level, you know that there is more to life for you. You know that you are capable of more. You know that more is normal for an infinite being such as yourself.

And you know the critic is standing between you and your more.

Be bold. Be brave. And be more in tune than I was. Stand in front of the mirror and stare down all your fears as you practice your new ideas.

To assist with this practice, let's add a few more ideas to your notebook. We will practice new ideas that help us practice our new ideas. That's what smart souls do. They create new ideas to help them get where they want to go. Here are the new ideas:

- I easily and effortlessly practice new ideas using a mirror, every day.

- I enjoy the process of saying nice things to myself and creating new thoughts to help me.
- I love looking into my eyes and practicing.
- I am willing to do this practice for the rest of my life to keep my fears at bay.

These ideas, if practiced, will help you remember to practice. These ideas, once entrenched, will create a daily habit of looking at yourself in the mirror and saying, *I love myself.* These ideas, if you add them to your practice, will make the practice easier for you.

I know this is hard. I know you will resist this. I know you will forget to do this, at first. So here is my offer. If you want to send me a message, I will remind you every day for thirty days to do your practice in front of a mirror. If you are into self-motivation, here are other ideas:

- Put a Post-it on the bathroom mirror that says "I am" and let it be your reminder to practice. Let it also be a cryptic message to your housemates that you are undergoing work on yourself, for yourself, and they could too.
- Create a reminder on your phone that you don't clear until you've been in front of the mirror and looked yourself in the eye. Use the clearing of the reminder as a reason to celebrate.
- Make a list of people you love and add everyone you can think of to the list, including yourself. Now, say this to the list: *I am practicing in front of the mirror so I can heal my fears. Once I go first, you will find that you want to go next, so I am doing this for all of you, whom I love, as much as I am doing it for me.*

- Ask for help from your spirit to remind you to practice. Be prepared to be surprised and delighted.
- Create a grid in your notebook, listing out the next thirty dates. Cross off each day once you do mirror work. Say, *Just as I am creating a chain of days of practice, I am creating a new, powerful chain of thoughts that will support me in all of life.*
- Write up your practice in an email and send it to yourself each day, for thirty days. When the email arrives, go find a mirror and practice.
- Create a new association between your car mirror and your practice. Get into the car and do your practice before you leave. Put a reminder note on your dashboard that covers the display screen so you can't leave until you practice.
- Press your friends to help you by asking them to text you every day and encourage you to do the work of losing your critic. Ask them to text fun and uplifting messages. They will get as much as you do out of the practice.
- If you are into more substantive technology work, create a video reel of your practice statements and play the reel as you practice, reading each statement as it comes up in the reel. Or develop a program that serves you practice statements, in differing orders, for your mirror work.

The mirror is your friend. It's literally you standing there, so I hope you see yourself as your own best friend. I hope you look into your eyes and notice a glimmer. I hope you stare into your eyes and see new possibilities. I hope you make the most of mirror work and cruise toward life without the critic.

TAKEAWAYS

- Mirror work works.
- Mirror work gets easier each time you do it.
- You can add in mirror work any time.

Ralph has his head in the clouds. He is daydreaming of how he could get the woman he wants if only he were taller, had more hair, and had a job that paid well. It's always been his lot in life, he thinks, that he is one of the ordinary people. And he would love to be spectacular. Ralph kicks at the dirt, his frustration growing. It just feels so unfair that he looks the way he looks. That he doesn't have natural charm. That he is someone who prefers to read than to do something more exciting that would be attractive to women. Ralph sees a young skateboarder up ahead on the park benches, an area that is clearly marked for no skateboarding. Ralph accelerates his step and gets ready to confront the young man, but he is off before Ralph can tell him off. *Damn skateboarders*, he mumbles to himself as he goes back to his thoughts about the woman he'll never get.

Ralph's critic is not only down on him, but he thinks that Ralph is predestined to be ordinary. Ralph would be well served to use a practice of self-love that embraces who he is today. His critic is giving him a little relief by pointing the criticism at others, but Ralph would find the greatest relief if he let go of the critic for good.

Day 10

YOUR WORDS MATTER

As you curate the new ideas you are practicing, I hope you find that your words hold power. Here is why I think your own words are your best healing source:

Your words are a reflection of your ideas. Your words are a tangible manifestation of your ideas. Your words are a form of communication, you to you. Your words are uniquely powerful in healing you.

On Day Five, we created a list of custom messages that we needed to hear. This list emanated from our list of transgressions and was created to dole out the messages of love we needed to heal up our past. I hope you are practicing these custom ideas. I hope you are standing in front of the mirror and telling yourself that you are good, you are loving, and you are worthy. I hope you see that your words hold great power over your own experience, so I want you to see that any negative self-talk you engage in is depleting your power and handing it over to the critic.

Negative self-talk would be easy to stop if we could only recognize the negative self-talk. Unfortunately, many of us have a habit of downplaying ourselves, which we hardly notice. Many of us have a learned response of self-denial that we think makes us humble. Many of us have limiting beliefs that say, *I should not say good things about myself to others.*

In fact, some think we are holy because we deflect, defer, and demean ourselves.

Your self-talk is one of the most powerful tools you have. With each word you use to describe yourself, you have the power to set yourself up for success or eviscerate your own confidence. You have so much power that you will resist changing your self-talk because you are worried that you won't know who you are if you claim your magnificence. Your patterns of self-denial may be so entrenched that you no longer see them.

We can often more easily see patterns in others than in ourselves. We notice when others hold themselves down or back, but rarely do we notice when we do it. So today's exercise is a little different. I ask you to think about a person you know or have observed who was self-sabotaging. I want you to think about a person who you view as having low self-esteem. I want you to remember a person who you think was playing small.

Before we get all hung up here, this isn't about judgment of that person. They are entitled to live their life however they want. But when another person helps you to see something about yourself, thank that person. Then turn your attention onto yourself.

With that out of the way, let's sit for a minute with the person you conjured up. How would you describe him? What does she wear?

What does he project into the world? What does she say about herself? I find it helpful to write these ideas down so I can better remember what is coming up for me.

You could write, *He never stands up straight*. Or *She is always a mess*. Or *He never speaks up in meetings*. Or *She has no boundaries*. Put it all on paper as you try to describe someone who you feel is not living up to their full potential. Who you believe is playing it safe. Who you think has a long way to go to claim themselves.

With each observation, I want you to thank that person for being a mirror for you. And then I want you to turn to your notebook to create new ideas.

What we notice and judge in another is often what we need for ourselves. And if you have a loud critic, you likely are using many other people as mirrors to deflect the perceived criticism of yourself. That's OK. That's normal. We are now going to send our friend off with our thanks and turn to our own inner work.

With your list of observations, write a list of attributes you want to be true for you. If you wrote, *She is bumbling when she speaks*, write, *I want to speak clearly and confidently*. If you wrote, *He is weak and small minded*, then write, *I want to be strong of mind and spirit*. If you wrote, *She looks like an unmade bed*, then write, *I want to look sharp and pulled together*.

Claiming your own wants is a skill for life. It should be taught in schools and refreshed in the workplace. We are suffering from an onslaught of people who don't know what they want, can't say what they want, or don't see that their judgments are hiding wants. And your critic is likely causing you to project all sorts of wants onto others.

Make your list of wants as long as you can. What else bothers you about people with low self-esteem? Go general and keep expanding your list. With each item you find that bothers you, turn to your notebook and harvest your personal want.

Before you stress out, this isn't about getting your wants today or launching a big personal improvement project. This is about honest expression. This is about noticing your wants. This is about noticing where you might not be owning your own desires.

When you say, "I want," you open doors inside you. The critic tries to race ahead and figure out how to get what you want. When the critic decides that it's not possible to get what you want, the critic looks for other people to judge. It's a pattern. You are noticing it. And you will eventually master it. But for today, we are practicing the art of noticing a want and doing nothing about that want except talking to ourselves differently.

If you wrote, *He never pursues his own agenda*, say, *I want to pursue my own agenda*. If you wrote, *She is too scared to leave her job*, write, *I want to leave my job*. If you judged, *He is too overweight*, then write, *I want to be fit*. This isn't about judging your wants. It's about listing them.

Saying "I want" is powerful. Often we obscure our own wants because we don't think they can come true. Our work today is to see that we have wants and that our expression—with our words—of those wants is valuable. For us.

This exercise is one way to help you turn around the critic. You are creating a new idea: a criticism hides a want. Then you are going one step further and harvesting that want, for yourself, so you can practice it with your words.

First you will say what you want. Then you will express an intention to get where you want to go. Then you will affirm the thing you want as if it already happened.

If you wrote in your notebook, *I want to present as a confident leader*, then you will say:

I intend to be more confident in how I present.

I am a confident leader.

As always, your words are your best tools. Try to phrase each part of the three-way process in your own words.

If you wrote, *I want to be more polished*, then you would follow that with:

I intend to present in a more polished way in the future.

I am polished and smart in my presentation.

If you wrote, *I want to stand up straighter*, then you will say:

I intend to improve my posture and claim my power.

I am powerfully in charge of how I carry myself.

This is about recognizing that criticism is always about a veiled want. This is also about practicing ideas that will help you feel more confident and self-assured.

A strong critic erodes our confidence. The critic tears us down because it thinks it is the right thing to do. It highlights our weaknesses, under a mistaken belief that fixing a weakness leads to success.

You now have the chance to upend the mistaken chain of thoughts that the critic offers. You will proudly claim what you want and celebrate that you have wants. You will then continue your mirror work with your new intentions and affirmations, and you will feel a sense of having what you want.

Wants are something to cherish. If you have wants for yourself, then you are alive. If you have wants, then your spirit is lively and energetic. If you have wants that you claim, then you are on the path to releasing the hold the critic has on you.

I told you that the critic could be useful. So here we are using the critic to help us find our own wants. That's a valuable exercise, in and of itself. When you couple that with the use of intentions and affirmations, then you zoom past the critic and right into the arms of the true you. Look into that mirror and see yourself as gifting yourself with these words. Say, if you can, *My words have power, and I am using them to invest in myself.*

Words, I have found, pay dividends if you choose them wisely. They also can contribute to your negative self-worth if you don't choose wisely. As you reflect on the words you use to describe yourself, I hope you see that you can add to the assets on your self-worth balance sheet, or you can create liabilities. One earns you interest. The other costs you interest. As you sink further and further into negative self-talk, you eventually lose interest. In life. In yourself. In your own good opinion.

Yet the opposite is equally true. The more you show up, say good things to yourself, and claim your wants, the more interesting life becomes. The more interesting you become. You set yourself on an upward, positive trajectory, and life is all the sweeter on the rise. Because you had the critic for so long, you will relish life without the critic. You, beautiful soul that you are, will shine brightly once you turn the tables on the critic and harvest your wants. You, savvy human that you are, will remember the days of the critic and celebrate that you overcame a thought pattern to better your own life.

TAKEAWAYS

- You can practice new ideas that benefit you.
- Allow your judgments of others to help you see the words you need to hear; give them to yourself.
- Invest in yourself with your words.

Damon cannot believe he is the first person at work today; that never happens to him. But he has turned over a new leaf, and he is going all in on his new routine. He got up at 5:00 a.m., he worked out, and now he is walking around the office, turning on the lights. Damon has a strict plan, and it involves every hour being planned out. He even meal-prepped over the weekend so he would be ready. Damon is following a new protocol that he learned from a friend, who guarantees it will turn Damon's life around. Damon is proud of himself for sticking to the regimen and is wondering when he will see results.

Damon's true self is not into protocols or rigid rules. That's his critic. Damon would enjoy a plan where he tapped into his inner wisdom and let the critic loose. There he would find routines and actions that worked for him.

Day 11

PERFECTION OF TODAY

Your practice is growing long, and you are awash in new ideas that you could practice. You appreciate the effectiveness of the practice and see how you can create new ideas. You might even have seen a shift in your thinking that suggests that better ideas are available to you all the time. And they are, but we will curate your list today so you can focus on a few ideas that will help you move quickly through the next stages of work.

Most of us with a loud critic are used to being shown what went wrong. We are accustomed to debriefing, dissecting, and demeaning what occurred so we can improve it for next time. Many of us have a propensity toward self-help and self-improvement, and we see it as a fun way to spend our time on earth, maximizing our full potential.

Maximizing your potential, as a goal, is worthy and good. A smart, savvy soul would want to have the best possible life experience. But here is where the critic jumps the tracks. The critic believes there is something fundamentally wrong with you. And that is the false premise we need to disentangle from your desire to improve.

As I said, a desire to improve is natural. Seems like a logical path for someone who wants to grow and learn. It also seems like a normal path for someone who is an eternal being. Aren't you always growing into more?

So, this desire is not wrong, bad, or a problem. The problem is that some people think they are improving to fix themselves, rather than seeing how improvement happens naturally once you accept your perfection as you are.

I use the word "perfection" carefully here because those of us with critics have a love-hate relationship with perfection. We love to strive for it. We hate when we can't get to it. Perfection, then, becomes our mistress and our nemesis. We both love the striving and hate the missing.

Perfection, I have found, is based on a false premise. It assumes that there is a point in time, in the future, when everything will be as it should. When all will be aligned, ordered, and fair. When all will be right, good, and just. And that idea—that perfection exists in the future—causes us to completely miss that perfection exists today. Right where we are.

You will resist this idea because that's what people with a critic do. They assume they are not perfect, the world is not perfect, and that life is not perfect. Which is why they strive. But perfection is simply an idea you created, which means you can uncreate, modify, and alter it to serve your purposes.

Embracing the perfection of today is like taking a cool drink of water on a hot, sunny day and realizing you are perfectly satisfied in that moment. It's like looking around the table at those you love over dinner and seeing that where you are, in that moment, is ideal. It's like creating a master plan for how your life will go and then turning over the plan to someone who has grander plans than you for what you can accomplish. And in that moment, you see that where you are is perfect.

I came into the idea of perfection of the present moment by practicing it. I simply decided that I was going to see life as perfect, right now, and then let what happened happen. I was afraid when I started this practice. I thought that seeing life as perfect meant I was settling for what is. I thought that saying life was perfect would go against a cosmic truth that everyone but me knew. I thought by claiming myself as perfect as I am, I would be committing a transgression against my own soul.

Now that I am on the other side of this work, I can testify that claiming life and yourself as perfect sets you up for outsized success. Embracing the perfection of the present moment helps you leverage all your resources to tackle your goals. Seeing life as perfect for everyone is a way to honor the independence and freedom of each soul alive today.

Your biggest block to seeing the perfection of your present situation is your critic, who has bombarded you with messages that say, *You need to change. You need to improve. You need to do better.* These messages cause you to think that you are broken, flawed, or in need of repair. Not true. You are simply a human, having an experience of life, and growing each day in love.

We listen to these critical messages because, on one level, we believe that if we don't improve, get better, or perform at higher levels, then we will miss out on life. We'll miss out on our personal potential. We'll miss out on who we were set to become. Yet the opposite is happening.

By listening to the critic and believing we are flawed, we are negating our true selves. By following along with these mistaken ideas that we need repair, we are distancing ourselves from our own spirits. By failing to claim ourselves as worthy and perfect, in the moment, we are missing an opportunity to move forward based on love, not fear.

The critic deals in fear. That's how it motivates. That's how it assesses life. That's what it pumps out, all day. Your soul, I hope you realize, deals only in love. Love of you, love of life, and love of where you are. Yet still it wants more from life. Leaning into your soul doesn't make you complacent. It makes you effective.

To get here, start a new practice of ideas that will set you up for success. These ideas are novel, which means they will feel weird at first. That's OK. You know how to do this. You know that within a few days, you'll feel more comfortable with these new ideas. You know that you can do this work.

- I am a powerful soul created in love.
- I am willing to see life as perfect, as it is.
- I am open to seeing myself as perfect, as I am.
- I am willing to embrace perfection as something that exists only in the present moment.
- I am willing to see that perfection exists today, and still, I want to grow, change, and experience more of life.
- I am ready to see perfection as an idea and that idea as one I can change.

That's it. That's all you will practice for the next few days. Use the mirror, and practice these new ideas. If it helps, write them out every day too. See yourself as a person who is doing an experiment to determine if love or fear are better motivators. You've done fear all your life. Now is the time to see if love can get the job done.

My belief in the power of love is not a wishy-washy way of viewing the world. It's based on my life, my observations, and my experience. Here is what I have found: When I am doing an activity I love, my energy is boundless. When I am engaged with a topic that interests me, I can work for hours without a break. When I am in the zone of something I am passionate about, I often work without stopping to eat. That's how powerful love is. It will literally propel you to do more than you thought possible.

Believing you are broken is exhausting. Thinking you are a problem to be solved is soul-crushing. Listening to the critic harangue you into taking action is not a long-term, sustainable plan for a life worth living.

We are breaking seriously old cycles of thinking here, so know that you may—upon first reading this—totally reject what I am saying. You may be so attuned to your critic that you don't believe perfection exists, and instead, you wallow in the imperfection of life. You may be so out of touch with your own soul that you think perfection is what happens after you die. You may be so entrenched in your belief in your brokenness that you have given up on trying to improve.

These are all signs of the critic run amok.

The critic is a pattern of thought, and you can break the pattern. You are doing so by cutting out from under the critic the fundamental belief that you are a problem. That you are flawed. That you are a soul unworthy of love, and thus, need to earn it. Once you clear out any idea that you are a problem, the critic loses its grip on you. Sure, you have ways that you want to improve. But they do not negate you, your perfection, or your goodness, as you exist today.

When this practice is embraced, you ease up on life. You come to life with an open hand that says, *I don't need to control everything. I can allow life to lead me along for a while. I can loosen my grip on the steering wheel and look around to see how beautiful life is today. I can relax into being me, as I am perfect as I am.*

I see this practice as surrender. It is surrender of your limiting beliefs around your brokenness. It is surrender of your mistaken idea that your creator could make something imperfect. It is surrender of your need to change life, in this moment, to be OK.

That's what the critic tells us: you must control everything around you to be at peace on the inside. Not true. Not possible. Not your work. Your work is only to tend to you, what you have going on in your head, and what you allow into your experience. I advocate that you allow these new ideas to take root in ways that bring you home. I suggest you practice these new ideas to help them grow. I am here to bear witness that these ideas, once practiced, can change how you work, how you perform, and what you can accomplish.

I am playing on your desire to maximize your full potential here to entice you to practice. Let me clear: I don't believe life requires anything of us. There are no mandates, no secret codes, and no demands. Just life, loving us, every day. But many of us have a true, burning desire to live up to our full potential, and that desire is best fueled by love, not fear.

TAKEAWAYS

- You are not a problem to be solved; you are a soul who wants to express.
- Practicing new ideas helps you to break free of old patterns of thought.
- You can maximize your full potential once you release the critic for good.

Elmer is tired of being the one who is always last. Always put upon. Always singled out. He grinds his teeth and vows that he will no longer allow people to overlook him. He comes forward in line and says to his boss, *I am not going to allow this anymore. I deserve to be treated better. I am not working the night shift, and I am not picking up hours that others don't want*. His boss is perplexed, mostly because he is not sure who Elmer is. But he responds, *OK*, and lets Elmer have his way. As Elmer walks away, his boss thinks, *That guy is angry; I need to keep an eye on him*.

Elmer would benefit from getting in touch with his authentic self, who already sees Elmer in all his glory. He would also benefit from becoming aware of his thinking and seeing how it affects him. His critic seems to think Elmer is small and overlooked and seeks to reinforce that. Elmer would be wise to stop listening to the critic and tune in elsewhere.

Day 12

LIFE WITHOUT THE CRITIC

Critics, left on their own, will take you down crazy paths. They'll spin out into worry, self-doubt, and self-negation. They might even push you into panic, fear, or anxiety. What they never do, however, is lift you up.

A critic's overarching goal is to keep you safe, and often that goal is accomplished by keeping you small. Smallness is something the critic can handle. The critic sees small and says, *That's enough. We can handle life if you stay small.*

What the critic can't handle is when you have big dreams. When you have ideas that are larger than you. When you have wants that seem to bypass all your fears and cause you to act.

When you hold a passion for a project, an idea, or even a person, it's as if your mind flies out the window, and your heart takes over. This is a scary place for the critic because the critic lives entirely as a figment of your own mind. Remember, the critic is nothing more than an idea, a thought pattern, and a way of reacting to life.

When you engage in activities you are passionate about, you can bypass the critic and simply get lost in the fun of doing something you love. Frankly, this is why I drink a glass of wine. It helps me let loose and seems to put my critic away for the night. It also helps me see what life could be without the critic, which is a life I see as worthy of my effort.

I never said losing the critic is easy; I simply said it can be done. What I want to paint for you is a picture of what that life is like so you can anticipate. I want to give you a sense of what life feels like when the critic is quiet. I want to help you anticipate the feeling place of living a critic-less life.

Life without the critic feels like I had a glass of wine, and now I am relaxed. Life without the critic feels like I can accomplish any goal I choose with ease. Life without the critic feels like a walk outside in the sun when the spring air is just warming up. It's glorious. It's delicious. And it's attainable.

To achieve life without the critic, you'll need to *want* to live a life without the critic. Yet most of us with giant critics don't even know we have the critic. We think it's just us, on the inside. We think we simply have a propensity to skew negative. We think we are hardwired to think about how things could go wrong. So there can be a fear that sets in, as you lose the critic, that feels like you are losing yourself. You are not. But it feels that way.

I want to prepare you for the backslide that can occur once you chip away at your critic. You may think, *I like how bitingly sarcastic I am.* Or *I enjoy my criticism of others; it makes me feel good.* Or *This is who I am; it's my personality.*

These ideas, which are all just fears, are not who you truly are on the inside. On the inside, you are smart, funny, lively, interested, and engaging. You like yourself. You enjoy your own company. You're fascinated by yourself. These are all the hallmarks of the authentic you.

What they tell us is that people who buy into the critic are buying into a story of who they are. All of us tell stories. We tell stories of who we are. We tell stories about what we witness. We tell stories of what we think other people are thinking. All stories. All made up. And all typical for being human.

What isn't typical, for those who do not have a critic, is to tell a story that casts you as the villain, the victim, or the underdog. Instead, those without a critic freely tell a story that casts them as the hero, as the savior, or as the winner. And they do it without a second thought as to the propriety of thinking of themselves so grandly.

This means that you, too, have an opportunity to tell a different story. And my goal is to get you passionate about your new life—your new story—without the critic.

To do this, we will reach for our notebook and write a story of what life would be like if we didn't second-guess ourselves. We will tell a tale of what life would be like if we focused on our successes. We will write, and rewrite, a story that helps us see that life without the critic is possible.

As you write of life without the critic, use examples to make it specific. Dig into your current day and look for examples of times when, if you didn't have the critic, you would have felt differently about the situation. This can be hard if the critic has a large place in your life. Hang in there and keep trying.

You could write how you felt decisive, confident, and at ease in a situation at work. You could write how you felt pretty, handsome, or good-looking as you dressed for the day. You could write how you overcame a challenge, conquered a goal, or made money from a project you love. You could write how you savored your dinner, were present with your family, and appreciated every aspect of the day.

When I do this, I imagine myself acting with choiceless ease, making one good decision after the other. I imagine myself doing work I love, and getting paid for it, all while the critic sits quietly on the sidelines. I imagine myself having great energy, good health, and fitness to help me feel good. In short, I imagine myself living my best life.

People with a critic are negative dreamers. We can make up details and scenarios as to what could go wrong, but when pressed to make up a positive story, we say, *I'm not creative.* Or *I don't think that way.* Or *That's not who I am.* Malarky. Those are all stories you have repeated, and it's time to take the skill you honed creating negative scenarios and use that skill to create positive dreams.

Imagine yourself doing something you are passionate about. You don't need to know what that is, but if you have a passion, picture yourself doing it. Picture yourself working for hours on that passion, having fun, laughing, and getting a lot accomplished. You might even imagine yourself telling someone how much fun you are having with your new project, even if you don't know what the project is. This is daydreaming, not scripting. You just need to get into the feeling of having something you are passionate about.

Your imagination could put you on a beach with your toes in the sand. Your mind could take you to a time you won a sporting event and experienced the fun of a win. You could be imagining a day when everything goes according to plan, and you feel the smoothness of a good day.

In your notebook, craft a story with your imagination. Write how you feel. Free. Independent. Sure-footed. Clever. Self-satisfied. Self-loving. Use any feeling that comes to mind and add it to your story. See yourself as having the best day you could imagine.

And now I will tell you that whatever you imagined, living without the critic is better. Whatever place you went to in your head to escape the critic, you can get there on a regular basis and thrive. Whatever feelings you conjured up with this practice, you can enjoy better feelings if you hang in there and keep up with the work of losing the critic.

Here's what does it for me. When I realized I could feel like I had a glass of wine without having one, just by using my imagination, I was hooked. When I realized I could feel a hum of excitement within me just by losing my critic for a few minutes, I became motivated to lose the critic. For good.

The title of this book has a dual meaning. Losing the critic is not only something you can do in a permanent way. It's something you can do for the greater good. For the benefit of all. No one benefits when you self-criticize. No one grows in love when you self-deny. No one becomes better off because someone they love holds themselves back.

That's how crazy a critic is. When you dream big, the critic will convince you that you will be leaving behind those you love if you soar high. When you step into your power, the critic will tell you that no one likes a person in power. When you embrace who you truly are, the critic will suggest that you are not interesting anymore. The critic will tell you that living a spirit-led life is boring, not for you, and too holy for your taste.

Let me disabuse you. A spirit-led life is fun, interesting, dynamic, loving, magnetic, and supercharged. It's good timing, overlaid with good ideas, mixed in with good people. It's full of laughs, surprises, and twists you did not see coming. It's a living, breathing relationship that you get to experience, you with you.

Your work, today, is to daydream. And this might be our hardest exercise yet. That's because the critic has told you that you aren't good at daydreaming. So I want you to recall a time you worried. The days you awaited a diagnosis, and you imagined the bad outcome, the loss of your hair, and the chemo treatments. The time you were convinced you would die, and you thought about how every loved one would react. The time you imagined your loved one in a horrific accident, maimed, or bleeding on the side of the road, all because she missed curfew. You are awesome at making things up. You, person with a critic, are superlative at embellishing details. You, human that you are, have a great mind for make-believe.

You are now going to use it to pretend you are living life without the critic. That you experience good luck, good timing, and good events, every day. That you feel good, energized, and on top of life. That you are winning, saving, and helping, all at the same time. You can do this, and it just takes practice.

What could help you is this. Write your day as if everything that happened went your way. Just recall your day, and then write each segment as if you were benefiting. Then, write the story again, seeking to make the benefits bigger, more awesome, more grandiose. Then, write it again, seeking to supersize it.

We are seeking to bypass the critic here, so the wilder your daydream, the better. This is an exercise of getting you into the feeling place of life being on your side. Which it is. But you can't see that because you are listening to the critic.

TAKEAWAYS

- Daydream what life will be like without the critic. Use that daydream to propel you forward.
- The true you is way more fun than your critic.

Patty has a great job. She has worked her way to the top, and she is now the manager of the entire office. It's something she has dreamed about since she started her career. She looks around her office and realizes that this is it. This is the final stop of her career. This is everything she worked for, but the victory seems hollow. She feels no thrill, no sense of excitement for the new role. She realizes, in an instant, that she feels tired, exhausted, and out of ideas. She doesn't even want to celebrate. She goes home and parks herself on the couch and feels a sense of emptiness.

Patty could benefit from losing her connection to the critic, who thinks that destinations matter more than the journey. Critics all around the world get this one wrong, and Patty will find, once she breaks free, that she is worthy of work that fulfills her, uplifts her, and makes her feel good about herself.

Day 13

USE A LOGBOOK

Yesterday, we began a process of daydreaming. This is atypical work for those of us with a critic, so be nice to yourself and say, *I am learning how to daydream in a positive way, and I'll get better with practice.*

Life is best improved in small doses, done daily. That's the nature of all the work in this book. You read, you do an exercise, you clear out blocks, you think differently. Then, you come back the next day and do it again.

What I have found helpful is a scorecard I can use to see my progress. Here, again, we will be working against the critic, so be forewarned that you might reject these ideas at first.

Most of us create lists of what we are supposed to do for the day. What we committed to do. What we think, in our mind, we must do. We make the list, often placing our hardest tasks at the top of the list to be tackled first. Many of us even have a game we play in which we can't feel satisfied until we cross off all the items on the list. We see the list as our master, and our adherence to the list as a sign of good discipline.

LOSE YOUR CRITIC FOR GOOD

This mode of working, which puts the focus on tasks you don't prefer to do, is so commonplace that there are websites and books on how to manage your to-do list. How to stop procrastinating on your to-do list. How to put the hammer down on your list and conquer your goals.

The critic often uses the task list to heap burdens on us. The critic sees only the undone, not the tasks completed. The critic chastises us for a task that hangs around on the list for too long. The critic sees completion as a good and moral act.

The task list has become fodder for the critic to run your life. And you are a far better manager of your own life than the critic is.

To circumvent the critic in this area, try a new process of list-making that ignores your task list and instead focuses solely on your accomplishments. You completely ignore what you *must do* and instead create lists of what you *did*. We will trash the task list, or at least place it on the back burner, and we will turn our attention to the process of logging our day.

You can use your existing notebook or get a fresh notebook to use for daily logging. With a new notebook, open to the front page and write, *This is my logbook, and here I will record the good, the wonderful, and the done so I may reorient my mind to look for the good, the wonderful, and the done.*

Now, turn to a fresh page and write today's date. Create a list of everything you accomplished today. You dressed and got ready for the day. You ate breakfast. You attended a meeting on climate regulation. Whatever you did, write it down. No, we aren't going to do this for the rest of your life, but we will do this for a week to create a new habit.

You can do this as granularly as you like. I recommend you start with natural segments. *E.g., I dropped the kids off at school. I made lunches.* Just reflect on your day and note all the things you did. Keep at it as you go about your day. Record your walk outside. List your phone call with your mom. Make a note of your errand purchasing new light bulbs. Just keep listing out what you do as you go about your day.

Then, express this intent: *I intend to notice what feels good to me.* You could write that at the top of your notebook as a reminder. As you work through your day, if you notice any good thing, write it down. You could note how traffic was light. You could note that no one complained about wearing their coat today. You could note that you felt particularly handsome in your new sweater. Just look for any good thing and note it.

If you feel like you need a task list to keep you on track, here is what I recommend. Make a list of all the things you think you need to do and then, next to each one, write exactly what you want. If you wrote a task that said, *Schedule dentist*, then next to that, write, *I want clean and healthy teeth.* If you have a task to pay your taxes, write, *I want to stay in compliance with the laws.* If you have a task to ask someone on a date, write, *I want a new romantic partner.* This isn't hard. Task plus want. Do this for every item you feel like you need to write down to remember to do.

Here is the funny thing about life: we don't forget to do things that we want to do. We might become distracted, but rarely do we forget to do something we enjoy. A task list, then, is a representation of activities that we don't want to do but feel are necessary to get what we want. Just note that for future reference.

LOSE YOUR CRITIC FOR GOOD

Your logbook is now your companion for the next week. Write down when you feel like you had good service at a restaurant. All you need to say is this: *Went out for tacos; great service.* You can do this with bullets, with stars, or in paragraphs. Totally up to you. The key is to write what you did and to collect anything that makes you feel good.

You'll forget this for half a day, and that's OK. Just spend a few minutes reflecting about the day, what you did, and what felt good. Get into the habit of noticing good feelings. Nice people. Helpful coworkers. Great design. Pretty flowers. Well-timed humor. Smooth pens. Excellent lighting. Good smells. Make a record of every positive thing in your day. And keep logging.

If you reach the end of the day and the critic is barking at you about what did not get done, pull out your logbook and read. See all the things you did get done. See all the good you found. And then say, *This is enough.*

Enough-ness is a belief you can cultivate, and you can begin, today, with a practice of saying, *I am enough.* I use that phrase when I feel the pull to do more than my energy is up for. I use that phrase when I enter a situation where I feel less than others. I use that phrase to tell my critic to back off.

Your logbook is more than just a pretty record of your days. It's a process to rewire your brain to look for the done and the good, every day. If you have been listening to your critic for a long time, then you are out of practice for this important life skill. If you have been running your life based on task lists, then you are likely not accustomed to stopping and celebrating what you did each day. If you have a habit of withholding self-love until the task list is complete, then you need to work hard to recode your brain to see that you are worthy of love no matter what you produce.

A logbook can become your faithful companion, if you allow it. Mine is sitting next to me on my desk as I write, and I will log, *Drafted a chapter for my book; felt so empowered*, when I am done. You can doodle in yours, create codes to categorize your day, or make lists in the book to keep you entertained. I like to notice when my family does things I don't expect or pitches in to help when I least expected it. I like to write down my accomplishments and when I felt strong, confident, and in charge. I like to collect good moments as if I am making deposits into my own investment account with each one.

A great use of your logbook is to record every exercise you do based on this book. A few days ago, I wrote, *Took a walk and supersized my daydreams in my imagination*. I also noted that I practiced new ideas (I am working on big goals). I also have an entry for creating a video to record my practice, something I encourage you to try. It's a great way to see yourself saying nice things to yourself.

The logbook has the power to change how you see the world. The logbook has the capacity to become a record of your every win, good moment, and good idea. The logbook, if you keep up with it, will change your life.

The logbook does not need to be in hard copy. I have digital lists and records of my best days. I use a notes app to capture what I want and know that the process of capturing is helping me create new pathways in my brain. What we capture is what we notice, and what we notice is what we experience. It's that simple.

If you do use a task list, see it as a recurring daily list that doesn't need to be completed today. I like to see mine as a "could-do" list. As in, *Here are items I could do if I had to.*

Of course, I have action items that need my attention. I have a job, family demands, and normal life requirements such as doctors, bills, and shopping. But I try not to live my life based on requirements. I try to live my life predominantly doing what I want.

Your logbook can become a record of all your best ideas. I jot down inspiration, quotes, or pithy sayings I unearth. Which is another benefit of losing the critic: you get inspired more and more.

The critic will go silent if you keep up the logbook. That's because the critic has no role in it. All you are doing is logging what you did and looking for good moments. That's it. We aren't assessing our performance, second-guessing our actions, or picking apart our days. We are logging and noticing. The critic has nothing to do.

TAKEAWAYS

- Logging your day is a power move that could flip your thinking in a rapid way.
- Use your logbook as a record of a life well lived.
- Your logbook can become whatever you choose. I hope you choose to fill it with moments you love.

Roberto never saw a shopping center that he didn't want to visit. It's as if the second he sees a store, he is drawn inside to buy things. He doesn't spend much. In fact, he is adept at getting the best deals, and always buys when things are on sale. His car is so full of bags that he can't remember their contents. At first, he stops himself before going in. He asks, *Do I need anything from here? Aren't I just contributing to the environmental problems?* He feels a tinge of remorse and then walks into the store, where he buys a box of stickers that are on sale, and he is sure someone he knows could use them.

Roberto's critic could be cut loose so Roberto could listen to himself and not what the critic has to say. Roberto's best path is to find activities he enjoys and then not beat himself up for doing them. Roberto could benefit from clearing his blocks to see why he buys things he does not want.

Day 14

OWN YOUR DAY

With your new logbook, you have a tool to make substantial progress toward your goal of changing your thought patterns. That's all we are doing: creating new habits of thought where you go to the positive as much as you go to the negative.

We aren't seeking to become a myopic fool who never sees bad in the world. We are seeking to create a habit of positive reflection that more closely aligns with our souls. So don't worry about your stray thoughts and regression into old habits of criticism. That's normal. We are simply helping you tip the balance toward more positive thinking about yourself and life, rather than incessant negative thinking.

Our next exercise is going to build on the logbook habit and cause you to develop a habit of starting your day based on a positive. Some of us have such strong critics that we wake up asking ourselves, *What do I have to do today?* Or we say, *I have to get up.* Or *I need to get moving.* These are all fear-based ideas that suggest we aren't in charge of our lives, which the critic loves. The critic loves to be in charge, so it will take any transfer of power we allow.

That's how I see *shoulds, musts, have tos*, and *ought tos*. They are a tiny transfer of power wherein you say, *I don't know what's best for me, so I am going to follow someone else's rule for how I live my life.* This power transfer adds up over time, and before you realize it, you are living life according to the *shoulds*. You ask yourself, *What should I do next?* You say to yourself, *Here is what I should be doing.* You look at others and think, *Here is what they should do.*

The *shoulds* are a habit of thought that plays into critic mentality. The critic loves rules, strict either-or situations, and hard edges. The critic does not play well with ambiguity, relativity, or even subjectivity. Thus, when you give your power away to the critic by pretending that the *shoulds* are in charge, the critic takes the power and runs with it.

We see this when the critic berates you for not doing what you should. We see this when the critic puts you into a thought loop trying to discern what you should do. (A pointless, infinite loop, by the way.) We see this when the critic demands perfect compliance with the *shoulds* as a way of keeping you safe.

To get out of a habit of looking to the *shoulds* to tell us how to live our lives, we will start our days with a new idea that reclaims our power from the get-go. You will brainstorm a phrase, a mantra, or even a word you can use—every day—upon waking to set the table for how your day will go. Then you can write that phrase in your logbook every day until it becomes a program that runs on default in the back of your brain.

In fact, see the critic as an old program that has been running unattended for years in your back brain. It is a program that says, *She must be controlled to be accepted.* It says, *He needs to follow all the rules to be loved.* It says, *She needs to keep herself small to avoid being struck down.* This is the crazy talk that the critic operates in your brain.

Let's take back your power by changing your programming. And that starts today. Your brainstormed list is going to contain ideas that you will generate, and then you will choose a catchphrase that you can use to start your day. Choose one that resonates with you. Choose one that makes you feel good. Choose one you can live with for a while, as we will practice this for the rest of this book. After that, I suspect you'll go into autopilot mode, and this new phrase will become a way of living for you. But first you need to practice it.

To help you discover your new phrase, here is my own personal list of ideas to start your day. We are looking for power statements that put you squarely in charge.

- I am powerfully ready to seize the day.
- I am in charge of me, and I am the best boss I know.
- I have a plan for my day, and I am ready to begin.
- I am taking today by storm.
- I am ready to create the life of my dreams.
- I can't wait to live my life.
- I am ready to win today.
- I have great ideas, and I am ready to unleash them into the world.
- I have a plan, and I am ready for action.
- I have great ideas, and I plan to follow my own guidance.
- I am.

- I am the superstar of my own production.
- I am the hero of my own story.
- I am ready to have the best day of my life so far.

These are ideas and suggestions. Play with the words, the cadence, and the feel. I am currently in a phase where I am having fun saying *I am about to take the day by storm* as I get out of bed, but I like levity to my self-talk. I also like a little drama, which always makes me smile.

Put your new catchphrase on repeat and have fun with it. It's a statement that helps you wake up and say, *I am in charge of my mind, my body, and my soul, and I am going to use all three to my best advantage today.*

Remember, the critic is a figment of the mind. Our work is to establish a catchphrase to anchor the day and make it a habit. It's a new pattern. Which means it will feel weird for a few days until it sinks in.

New thought patterns are like any other life habit. You set an intent to change your habit. You give yourself reminders to help make the new activity a routine. And then, eventually, it goes on autopilot. So be ready for a bumpy first week, and plan for an eventual settling in that is automatic.

New, positive ideas are like fish bait. Once you drop crumbs of food, your inner being comes forward to gobble up the new, positive ideas. Soon she becomes used to the new positive statements and looks for even better ideas. You might start with a mantra that says, *I am in charge of me*, and by the end of the month, you are saying, *I am a powerful creator of the best day ever.*

You have a long history with the critic, so it's not going away overnight. But here is where I want to encourage you to take any step toward positivity you can find. When I take action to affirmatively change my self-talk, it's as if my own spirit swoops in and helps me move ahead more quickly. I can't explain it, but one positive thought begets ten more positive thoughts. And there is a momentum to the tiny habits you are creating.

A morning catchphrase may seem simple, but it is a powerful way to start your day. It's a step in the right direction and, for me, often leads to more and more positive thoughts that come in behind the first positive thought of the day. Plus, it makes me feel more powerful, which is always a great position to be in when the critic barks.

And the critic will bark. Don't worry about it. Don't fret. Don't even get worked up about it. Instead, see the critic as a vestige of an outdated way of living. The critic is from another time, when you were misinformed about your need for a critic. Now you know better.

We've excavated our reasons for creating the critic, and one that looms large for many of us is the goodness of being a rule follower. Rules are part of life, and you would be wise to be aware of them. I'm a lawyer who deals in rules, so I have a healthy understanding of how they benefit us. But here is my best advice: see yourself as a rule snob. An elitist when it comes to rules. Decide that you are willing to allow rules that help you succeed in life, but you aren't going to take in rules that make you feel inferior, less than, or worthless. Decide to weed out rules that place burdens on you that you do not want, create responsibilities you aren't willing to take, or mask your true underlying wants from yourself.

Our society is nothing more than a web of rules. With the internet, we are faced with more rules every day. How we are supposed to look. How we are supposed to act. How we are supposed to love.

Your work is to notice the rules you have implicitly adopted and question whether they are helpful to you, or to society in general. Is it a rule worth dying for? Is it a rule worth giving away your power to? Because every rule you buy into becomes ammunition for the critic.

The critic's weapon is scrutiny. It scrutinizes your every behavior to see if it complies with the rules. If you believe in the rule, then your variance becomes a basis for extended self-criticism. If you reject the rule, however, now you stand a chance of freedom from the backlash of the critic.

Many of the rules we allow into our lives are nonsense. They are rules around what we are supposed to say to people, how we are supposed to behave, and whom we get to love. I am now careful with any rule I allow in because I want a life free of the critic's nonsensical and strict compliance with ideas that aren't even my own.

As I said, I see a place for rules. They help us all get along. But when those rules overextend into our daily lives, then I have a rule: I only adopt rules of thumb, not rules. That's how I navigate society. I see all those rules as rules of thumb, which I can take or leave, not strict requirements. I adopt rules of thumb that help me in life and reject those that don't. I see every rule as having exceptions, and I seek to find balance in any rule that I let in.

Those without a critic may not have this problem with rules. But if you have a critic, you could have an unhealthy relationship with rules that keeps you stuck, in negative thought loops, or unaware. My best advice: be judicious in the rules you embrace.

Start your day with neither a rule nor a question. Start your day with a declaration of your power, your position in charge, and your positive expectation for the day.

TAKEAWAYS

- Start your day in your power, not in your head, meandering around ideas of what you are required to do.
- Be a rule snob.
- Your inner being doesn't need any rules.

Tasha has a problem. She is never going to find a mate, and she is tired of looking. She tells her mother that it's not in the cards for her and then proceeds to delete every dating app from her phone as a way of signaling she is done for good. The next day, she receives a message from a friend, asking to set her up with someone new. Tasha sighs and takes a moment before replying. She doesn't want to be set up, but she also doesn't want to disappoint her friend. She sends off a reluctant yes, with the hopes that the date never comes to fruition. Tasha goes into the kitchen and eats, as that is the only place she feels at peace.

Tasha's critic has crazy ideas that say her life is supposed to be lived as other people expect her to live. She could benefit from a decision to let go of the critic and listen only to herself.

Day 15

EMBRACE THE LULL

Once you lose your critic, you go into this phase that feels like a funk. It's not a funk; it's just a brief transitory phase where you are breaking the habit of using fear as a motivator, waiting for your natural motivators to kick in. Remember fear motivators? When you work to a deadline set by someone else. When you work on projects dictated by others. When you do things you think you should, rather than honoring what you want. Those are fear motivators that emanate from the critic.

Once you see fear motivators, you lose your taste for them. They feel like a bad idea. They feel oppressive. They feel like someone else is trying to boss you around. And they are, but you have a habit of letting them.

Using criticism to make yourself do things is the epitome of a fear-based motivator. It essentially says, *I am not able to know or decide for myself, so I will let someone else determine my worth*. It is a statement that says, *I don't trust myself to do what is best for me, so I leave it to others to define what is best for me.* It's an idea that undercuts your value as a human being.

Many of us use criticism to push us toward our goals. We rally ourselves by saying, *Don't be so lazy; get moving.* We push ourselves forward by saying, *I don't want to be a loser or suffer failure.* We regale ourselves with stories of how terrifying it would be to fail. That's all fear, and it's a fickle mistress.

Fear gets you only so far. Sure, it might get you to the gym, but real and lasting change comes only when you find something you love. It might force you to do something you didn't think was possible, but if you aren't in love with what you do, then what's the point? It could be a short-term fix to help you jump-start something bigger, but you want sustainable change, not flash-in-the-pan results.

Losing your critic is about losing fear as a motivator. And when you do that, you enter this lull phase where you feel like there is nothing you want to do. That's not true, but it feels that way. I want you to be prepared for the lull.

The lull is nothing more than a neutral spot where you are transitioning from taking action out of fear (taking action because you should or because you are meeting others' expectations) to taking action because you have a want. We are headed for a place where you do things because you want to do them, most of the time. We are driving toward a reality where you take action because you are interested or passionate. We are creating a new life where you do things that make you feel good. That's just a flavor of where we are going. But we must pass through the lull.

The lull is the moment when you realize that taking action out of fear is no longer for you. You won't be bullied into doing something just because someone says you should, and you no longer force yourself to do things you don't want to do. This is where the lull is essential and can be fun, if you allow it.

The lull, as I said, feels like you have no wants. You do, but they are in hiding. You have repressed your true wants for so long, because you were doing what was expected of you to keep the critic quiet, that your wants feel inaccessible. They are there, but they aren't top of mind. They exist, but they aren't accustomed to coming forward. They are there for you, but you might need to coax them forward.

During the lull, you could feel lethargic, low on energy, or even bored. You could feel lazy, out of sorts, and at your wits' end. That's because many of us with a critic have a habit of doing to avoid the wrath of the critic. It's easier to keep moving than to sit with introspection of how you have failed, screwed up, or done wrong. It's easier to remain distracted than to do any real, productive thinking. It's easier to do what is expected of you than to suffer the criticism that you are selfish or egotistical for having your own wants.

The lull is best met with patience, kindness, and an attitude that says, *Now is the time for me to catch up on TV*. Most of us with critics don't do much relaxing, chilling out, or even simply being quiet and still, and this lull is your opportunity to catch up on everything you missed. But you will hate the lull, at first.

You'll hate the lull because you have a habit of thinking that says, *If I am doing, producing, or making money, then the critic has to back off.* You have thought loops that say, *I get to reward myself when I have done good for another*. You have ideas that say, *I am worthy of love because I completed a bunch of tasks*.

That was the old way of being, and you are entering a new way of being. One that makes self-love unconditional and productivity optional. One that tells you, *You are worthy exactly as you are, and you can change if you want.* One that embraces you exactly as you are and tells you that you can become more if you choose.

To prepare you for the lull where your wants are still waiting in the wings, practice a few new ideas to get ready. Here they are:

- I am allowing my wants to come forward, and that takes time, stillness, and relaxation.
- I will not criticize myself for going into the lull, which is a positive step forward out of fear.
- I will enjoy the lull and use it to stock up on downtime.

Here is a way to use your attachment to tasks to help you: create a new task where you take credit every time you do something mindless and fun. We will give ourselves a point every time we laze around. We will self-talk our way through the lull by saying kind and affirming things that knock the critic right off its perch.

When you reach the lull, and you feel like you have no desire to do anything, use a self-talk conversation that goes like this:

Well, I have hit the lull. Hooray! That means I am heading in the right direction. I know I have wants. I know they will emerge, and I am glad for this time of indecision or uncertainty to allow me an opportunity to just be. I enjoy taking time for myself and showering myself with praise. I enjoy taking action that feels pleasurable to me and allowing myself time to transition from fear motivators. I love where I am headed, and I will enjoy this lull while it lasts.

That's how I do self-talk now. I previously let my mind wander on its own, and it tended to serve me up things like this when I tried to relax:

What have you accomplished today? You aren't doing anything. What should you be doing now? You would feel better if you did more. You aren't getting better by watching TV. Why are you on your phone? You shouldn't have eaten that earlier. You are so bloated. You could lose weight if you were disciplined and tried harder. You have no internal motivation. You need someone else to make you do things so you can have a better life. You need a deadline and an accountability partner.

Notice the difference? One uplifts, the other depresses. One inspires, the other demotivates. One has you moving forward, the other has you stuck.

To move away from the negative self-talk—the critic—you pass through the lull. And you, because you are smart and savvy, are prepared. You will hit a free Saturday, or take a day off for yourself, and realize you have no idea what you want from the day. You'll panic a little as you think, *I am a barren wasteland of internal motivations and wants.* But then you will remember the lull, you'll snap out of it, and you will use all the tools above to help you navigate the lull days.

The lull came and went for me. It would appear for a few days, disappear, and then come back again. Now, I see life coming to me in cycles that move me two steps ahead and one step back. The lull was no different. On my down days, I embraced the lull. I found shows to binge. I sat outside and stared at nature. I played on my phone and looked for mindless games. I took baths. Once I get better at lulling, I scheduled spa days. I went to the pool in the summer. I stood by the fire in the winter and simply allowed myself to be.

As the lull passed, my internal motivation grew. I woke each day with a sense of purpose and a desire to do what I wanted first. I was no longer willing to squander my early morning hours doing something I thought I should. I reserved that precious time for what I wanted. Which, for me, was writing. I crafted a newsletter. I started a blog. I began creating courses based on my writing. And then I created this book. All while I worked my same full-time job. All while I still took care of my family. All while I had lull days interspersed.

Here's the bottom line: internal motivation is unstoppable.

Here is where your disbelief may hurt you. You may be so disconnected from your wants that you read this and think, *Well, that's not me. I have nothing like that in my life.* If you are there, then here is my best advice. What's the downside to pretending? Why not create an experiment where you practice saying, *I have an internal motivation that is on fire*, and then see what happens. Will you be worse off? Will you be less happy?

Here is my own personal view: we all have God-given internal motivators that are in there waiting to launch. We all have a fire in our belly for something, if we would only let it emerge. We all could find an activity that we love and would do for hours for free.

You aren't quitting your job (yet) or changing your life. We are walking you through a process of losing fear and criticism as motivators, and then opening the door for your interests, wants, and passions to walk through. And they will walk in if you hold the door open. The lull is you holding the door.

Embrace the lull. If you do this work, you will end up with more ideas, more inspiration, and more activities that you want to do than you ever had before, which will make the lull seem appealing. The lull is a passage, and you are prepared.

TAKEAWAYS

- Be prepared for the lull and embrace it as a fun transition in life.
- Once your true wants emerge, you will be more productive and busier than you ever thought possible. And you'll be loving life.
- The lull can be seen as a reclamation project where you are waiting for all your parts to catch up to you. Celebrate the homecoming.

Paul never has enough money to pay his bills. He gets a new credit card and uses it to pay off the old cards, thereby shifting his debt into the future. It's exhausting, and he knows it won't last. Paul lies awake at night, wondering how he got to this place and what is wrong with him for being so broke all the time. He knows that the end is coming, and his precarious house of cards is about to fall, but he doesn't know what to do. Paul reminds himself that he caused this mess, and thus, he must be the one to clean it up. He tosses and turns until his alarm goes off, and he gets up to head to work.

Paul has a love-hate relationship with the critic. He thinks the critic is helping him overcome his debt problems, but he feels lousy when he engages with the critic. Paul could release the critic and find that he has a loving inner wisdom that could help him find peace.

Day 16

CLEAR THE BLOCKS

We have perfected the process of emptying out our fears, limiting beliefs, and old, mistaken ideas. That process, which I detailed on Day Five, was a process of loving up your past selves and accepting yourself as you are and as you were. That process, which is a process to embrace for the rest of your life, helps you make peace within yourself, which fortifies you to deal with the critic. Now, take that process one step further, and let's work on consciously clearing our blocks that keep the critic around.

To do this, get a large pad of paper and still yourself. Empty out your mind of every reason why the critic is part of your life that you can think of. This process could take an hour or more, so set aside time for this first excavation. That's all we are doing. Digging up old ideas that are kicking around in your subconscious mind, and then deciding to choose new ideas. Each time you do this process of excavation, it will become easier, more light-inducing, and more effective. This first go-round, then, is our hardest one, but even this one will feel good once you are finished.

On your pad of paper, write, *Here are all the reasons I have a critic.* As I told you at the start, there are good reasons that we create a critic, and those reasons have staying power. Your goal is to excavate these reasons so that you can loosen the hold the critic has on you.

To begin, set an intention to quiet your mind and allow every idea that needs to be healed to come forward. Then, write, in a stream of consciousness, every idea that comes forward. You could unearth the idea that you think people with a critic are more successful. You could realize that you believe that the critic is helping you in life. You could uncover that you think the critic is the true you.

We have built up to be ready for this work, so you now know that the critic is not the true you. The true you, eternal being that you are, is a being made in love. The critic is a thought form based on fear. Yes, you have listened to the critic for a long time, and yes, you have old patterns of thought that push you into a critical mindset, but the critic is not you.

The true you is lighthearted, in love with life, and enjoying life. The true you is the person you are when no one is looking. The true you is the essence that is you when you light up.

We all have down days. But we also all have had moments when we were alight. Moments in life when we felt alive. Moments when we felt unstoppable. Those are the moments of the true you.

A long relationship with a critic may have caused you to forget about those moments, or even to fear them as not repeatable. Now is the time to reach into your memory bank for any moment when you felt alive.

For some, that time was during childhood, when we had free days and played for hours at a time. For others, it's when we get into a car and drive at top speed, weaving through traffic. For still others, it's the moment when we look around the dinner table and see those we love and feel happy. These are all moments of aliveness, and that's what your life is supposed to feel like.

As you unearth all the reasons you still have a critic, let any idea come forward, even if it seems silly or nonsensical. We are not judging these reasons. We are emptying ourselves of the reasons that the critic still exists.

You may think that your value is tied to being critical. You may think that you help people when you criticize them. You may think that you need to be critical to be taken seriously. Get all those ideas out of your head, and let them see daylight on the page.

Our background thoughts are often running the show in life, so a regular practice of emptying yourself is a good one to keep the background thoughts as supporting actors and not the stars of your show. You, awesome soul that you are, are the superstar in your own production, so it's time to play the part of the lead in your life.

It helps me to tell the critic that it is not in charge. I am. It also helps when I empty myself of reasons that the critic is part of my experience as a way of healing up my mind.

As you write pages and pages of reasons why fear has motivated you, you could discover that you think fear is necessary in life. You could unearth the idea that fear is a good thing. You could discover that you have a taste for fear because you use it so often to motivate you.

I personally had a long breakup with fear because I had this odd idea that fear kept me safe. That fear served a good purpose by keeping me from making a fool of myself. That fear was useful to tell me where I wasn't supposed to go with my life.

Now that I am on the other side, I see fear as a part of life, but not a necessary one. It's a useful indicator when my thinking goes off the rails, but beyond that, it's not helpful. In fact, I see fear as my own personal biggest block to full soul expression.

When I redo this exercise of emptying myself, I find new little nuggets that I didn't know were there. I might realize that I think the critic makes me funny. Or I could discover that losing the critic feels like a mountain too high to scale. Or I could excavate a limiting belief that says, *I am meant to have a critic for life.*

I believe in the power of infinite possibilities, so I don't get hung up on ideas that say, *This is how life is meant to be for me.* I do not see myself as destined to have a critic. In fact, I now see myself as blessed to have had the critic, so that I could experience the ridiculous sweetness of living a life without one.

As if all of life were one giant production, all designed to deliver me to the place where I am today.

Your work, today, is going to be difficult but highly beneficial. You are not yet practiced in letting your mind pour out of you, but it will get easier with each time you do it. Just keep writing until you have no more reasons. Feel free to repeat reasons or to have variations on the same reason. Those are thoughts coming in on the back of thoughts, and it's good to air them out.

You could write, *The critic is the smartest person in the room.* Or you could say, *The world needs me to be critical to ferret out what is wrong.* Or you could write, *I want to be critical, as it's fun.*

Put it all out there. No one is judging you. No reason is right; no reason is wrong. We are simply looking at how your mind operates, which is always a fascinating endeavor.

I think it's normal that we are each our own favorite subject. I think it's healthy that we each prefer ourselves. I think it's part of our shared humanity that we all love to talk about ourselves and our accomplishments. See this exercise as getting a window into the mind that is yours. See it as a decluttering project where you can't move forward until you deal with all your crap. See it as a massive action you can take every day to help you level up your life.

Clearing blocks is the work of a lifetime, so you may as well get good at it, starting today. If you wait until tomorrow, you'll just start at square one. Today is a great day to take the reins of your life and see what your mind is thinking.

Any thought that comes forward is a worthy thought to write down. You may have thoughts that have nothing to do with the critic. Put them down. You may spiral off into an entirely new download of thoughts, and your best path is to go with the flow and put it all out on paper. You will get so good at this that you will marvel that you accomplished anything in life with so much garbage kicking around in your head.

This exercise, which I avoided for years, was the single biggest jump I had in my distance from the critic. The more I did this, the more I found that the reasons for the critic to exist were silly and nonsensical and simply no longer motivated me. Ironically, it was the critic who kept me from this excavation work.

When you live with a critic, you avoid doing inner work because you expect a barrage of criticism. It's that simple. You develop this habit, born of a desire to defend yourself, of not engaging the critic because you no longer want to hear the critique. But the critic is there, in the background, running scripts. The best course of action is to release all those thoughts and let them see daylight.

Once you do this exercise, I want you to take a good long break and do something nice for yourself. I want you to thank yourself for showing up to do this work. I want you to say, *I am so glad that I can now see my thinking so I can choose to change my thinking.*

Tomorrow, we will use your list of reasons to create a turnaround script. For today, see yourself as emptying out the closets so you can put yourself to rights, back on the path of love.

TAKEAWAYS

- Often, our subconscious mind is full of ideas we don't believe; emptying them helps you remove them.
- Inner work is easy and is always loving.
- You have the power to clear your own blocks by emptying yourself of any idea that holds you back.

Jonathan has no issue with his work but feels like everything could go more smoothly if people just listened to him. He seems to be able to see and appreciate every kink in the process and knows what needs to happen to fix it. It's just that no one gives his ideas any credence. So Jonathan has stopped sharing them, but he hasn't stopped simmering in the background. He once sat through an entire meeting where the PowerPoint presentation wouldn't load, and he knew how to fix it, but no one asked him, so he kept his mouth shut. He thinks everyone is less smart than he is, and he takes satisfaction from that.

Jonathan is letting the critic keep him from expressing himself, which is leading to all sorts of masking behaviors. He would be wise to confront his limiting beliefs and get in touch with his authentic self to find a way to feel more empowered, more heard, and more in love with his own life.

Day 17

CRAFTING A TURNAROUND

Yesterday we emptied ourselves of reasons why we created the critic, kept the critic, and allowed the critic. Today we will use those reasons to heal our thinking.

Your list, I hope, is long and represents every idea you can come up with about why you have a critic in your life. If you think of more reasons, add them to your list.

This exercise, which you will do every other day for the next two weeks, is designed to help you dig deep into your thinking, which might have been lazy thinking. We all have lazy-thinking days, where we allow thoughts to carry us along in life without examining them. If you are someone who has never confronted her own thinking before, this will feel odd. But it will get easier, I promise.

For me, this process continued until I got to a place where the reasons would come forward, and I would immediately say, *Not true*. As in, I don't believe that. I just allowed that thought to take up space in my brain, but it's not what I truly believe.

What I believe is that taking action in love is far more satisfying and productive than taking action in fear. What I believe is that a life doing things you love is better than a life doing things because you should. What I believe is that all of us are fully equipped to heal ourselves, with our spirit by our side.

If yesterday's exercise brought up powerful and charged memories, please see someone to talk about that. If you are spiraling in shame, blame, and guilt, know that a trusted counselor will help you though those emotions and those thoughts. If you feel that you are alone with this work, reach out to anyone you love, and say, *I am working through things, and I'd like to be held.*

Our reasons for the critic often put us into a cycle of self-criticism, so be mindful of that. You need not criticize yourself for having a critic. It's nothing to be ashamed of, worried about, or even a problem. You are ready to move into a more effective way of living your life. Again, the critic isn't bad; it's simply misinformed.

To reform the mistaken ideas of our critic, we use our list of reasons that we downloaded yesterday to create a custom script, which we will practice, to help us adopt turnaround ideas. Turnaround ideas are ideas that you need to heal. Turnaround ideas are custom-created by you, for you. Turnaround ideas are a gift that you give yourself.

To create a turnaround idea, write the opposite of the reason you gave for why the critic exists. If you wrote, *The critic is excellent at noticing*, then you write, *I am excellent at noticing, and I don't need a critic for that*. If you wrote, *The critic keeps me from failing*, then you write, *I am successful without the critic*. If you wrote, *The critic makes me laugh*, then write, *I enjoy my own humor, thank you very much.*

We are, idea by idea, dismantling your attachment to the critic. We are taking aim at every silly belief you hold, including your ideas that fear makes you safe. We are tackling all your reasons, and then we are creating new ideas that combat them. This work is so powerful that you will be able to use it to clear any block you have in your life.

If you wrote, *The critic helps me see what is wrong*, then you write, *I want to see that which is going well.* If you wrote, *The critic has great ideas of how to improve things*, then you write, *I am perfectly capable of leading my own life.* If you wrote, *The critic helps me be more efficient*, then you write, *The critic slows me down; my spirit speeds me up.*

Remember, the critic is just an idea. You are creating new ideas that chip away at the idea of a critic. That's all. And you are doing it so you can embrace a life where you do what you want and no longer check in with the critic to make your decisions.

That's how some live. We caucus with others to get their viewpoints on what we should do. We search incessantly online for answers on how we should live our lives. We search for role models and then try to emulate their routines or conduct. These are all ways that the critic has tricked us into giving our power away.

You, powerful soul that you are, are best positioned to lead your life. You, glorious human that you are, are the person who has the most vested interest in leading a good life. You, person who has a critic, didn't know that the true you stands ready to lead you into the light.

I believe that every person can do this work, whether they believe in their spirit or not. But here is what I have experienced: as I welcomed in my spirit to help me in life, including with my critic, I made progress by leaps and bounds. I flipped the script so completely that my critic now feels like a vestige of another lifetime. I fell so in love with myself and my spirit that I no longer care what anyone thinks.

That's what this new script can do for you. As you work through your reasons, have fun with your turnaround statements. Make them feel lighthearted or funny. If you feel strongly that a reason on the list is wrong, say, "Not true!" and then write what you believe. Get into the good feeling of knocking out every errant thought that has weighed you down.

That's what the list of reasons is: dead weight. They are misinformed ideas that kept you tethered to the critic. Now is your chance to unwind the past, undo your thinking, and choose to move to a more loving way of being in the world.

As you craft your new script, you'll invariably encounter a reason that you think is still a good reason to have the critic. That's OK. Ideas get changed all the time, so see this as your opportunity to try on a new idea. Write out the opposite, and make it a point to give extra attention to that new idea.

New ideas come into our lives every single day. See this as a blessing. See new ideas as new opportunities. They allow you to say, *Am I going to cling to my old, narrow way of seeing the world, or am I ready for a broadened and expanded belief?* You choose. You do it on a subconscious level, and now we are choosing with awareness.

As you clear out the dead weight, you will feel lighter. I see this as my natural inner light raising me up. I don't have to work on that; I simply allow that. And my new script helps me move into a place of allowing.

Your new script is your work for today. Stand in front of a mirror, look yourself in the eye, and then read your new ideas. If you feel uncomfortable, say, *I am worthy of this work on myself.* If you feel afraid, say, *I release any fear, and I am ready to set myself up for success.* And if you feel like you don't like what you see in the mirror, then tell the critic to back off, as you have important work to do in loving yourself.

Saying a new script to yourself is brave, conscious, and smart. Practicing new ideas is the path out of the dark forest that the critic has kept you in. Creating a custom script, for you and by you, is the best way I have found to quash the inner demons.

We all have inner demons. Stuff roiling around inside of us that feels like a mess. Don't sweat it. You aren't any different than anyone else, no matter what the critic has told you. You're a human, with a bunch of fears and screwy thoughts. Now's the time to take charge and plant seeds of love.

That's what positive ideas are. Literal seeds in your mind that will grow if you allow them. They are revolutionary new ideas that are so potent, you fear them. And that fear is showing you that you have a giant want.

Here is what I have learned: I only fear what I truly want.

When I am indifferent about an activity or an idea, it gets no notice by me. I don't stew in worry about it. I don't latch on to it and wonder whether it's true. I bypass the idea entirely and move on with my life.

When an idea is for me, I can—at times—experience fear. Meaning, I want this to be true, and I want it so much that I am scared that it's not true. This often plays out in our desire to believe good things about ourselves. We want that, at a soul level, so clearly that we fear finding out it isn't true. If you are experiencing this sort of fear with your new ideas—fear that seems to hide a yearning or want—I want you to simply and matter-of-factly say, *Well, all this fear is showing me that I have a true want. Better to move toward the want.*

Your script can be read as many times as you want. There aren't rules on this. I try to read my script at least once per day, and then do a new clearing on the next day. I am now in a cycle of clearing and creating the new script at the same time. This happens when I unearth a block, and I immediately write down the turnaround statement right next to it, as a way of saying, *I don't believe the block. Here is what I truly believe.*

Practicing the turnaround statements is an action of great power. It's a mental activity where you recode yourself to think new things. Which is a nifty life trick. You can, with minimal effort, change what you believe. You can, with just a few days of practicing, think new thoughts. You can, with minimal investment, reap the benefits of being more aligned with your inner being.

When I feel aligned with my own soul, I light up. I feel positive, excited, and ready to take on the day. I feel uplifted, loving, and powerfully in charge of life. I feel like I have energy for days and that any goal is achievable. These are the feelings we want to generate in you.

Your turnaround script, if this is your first time through this book, is going to feel weird. We've been there before. You know how this works. You know the first time you say a new idea it feels silly. And within a week, it feels like raw power in your hands. Hang in there, do your practice, and clear every other day while you finish this book.

As I said, clearing can be used for any area of your life. Our focus is on dislodging the critic from your belief system. Here are positive beliefs that helped me break free:

- The critic is not me. It's an idea, nothing more.

- The critic is not helping me. It leads me into situations where I give my power away.
- The critic can't match the productivity levels of acting in love.
- The critic is a relic of past times; I am ready to move forward with a more modern view.
- The critic isn't a problem. It's an opportunity for me to say the opposite.
- The critic, if used for good, can become your best ally.

TAKEAWAYS

- Your blocks contain the words, or the idea, that you could practice to dissolve the block.
- Your custom-designed script will be exactly what you need.
- You have the power to turn around any belief that no longer serves you.

Barbara thinks her teenagers are the light of her life. But she just can't get them to do what she wants. Their rooms are a mess. Their sports equipment is everywhere. Their schoolbooks are covering the dining room table. And their laundry sits in baskets, folded and ready for them to take it to their rooms, but no one picks it up. Barbara is at a loss about what to do and whether she is giving her teenagers the best mothering. She worries that they aren't being the people she expects them to be and about whether she will be seen as a bad mother because of their conduct.

Barbara's critic has convinced her that her life is supposed to be about her children and not about her. Barbara could benefit from letting go of these ideas and centering on herself, her wants, and her feelings.

Day 18

LEVERAGE THE BACKLASH

Your new script is your custom prescription to bust through the limiting beliefs that you hold around having a critic. The script, if practiced, can easily take root and take on a life of its own. That's how new beliefs work: when you adopt positive, uplifting beliefs, you are amazed by how high they can take you.

My work in dealing with the critic may never be fully over. I say this not to discourage you, but to set the stage for what I call the backlash. The backlash occurs when you create new ideas that are counter to your current beliefs, and there's an internal struggle to see who wins.

I have seen this over and over in my life, so let me explain how it works. You practice new ideas that are beliefs you know will help you achieve greater levels of success. You know they are in you somewhere, just waiting to bust out. And in that creation of the new idea, life seems to serve you experiences to help you affirm your new belief. But that experience will feel like you are taking a step backward.

I want you to be prepared, so I will provide lots of examples here.

- If you practice saying, *Fear is unnecessary*, then you could have a life experience that serves you fear, and you get to confront that fear and say, *I don't need fear to accomplish my goals.*
- If you say, *I want to be done with the critic*, life may give you an experience where the critic is loud, so you can affirm, *I am ready to move on from the critic.*
- If you tell yourself, *The critic is not a way to run my life*, you could face an experience where your critical side will try to take the lead, and you get to tell it, *I am not doing that anymore.*
- If you have a new idea that says, *Love is a better motivator than fear*, then you could find yourself taking an action out of fear and stop yourself and say, *That's not how I want to move forward.*
- If you are carrying a new idea that says, *We don't need to self-criticize*, you could find yourself in an experience where you normally self-criticize, but it's your chance to stop that habit.
- If you are trying out a new idea that says, *The critic is no longer in charge*, then you might feel an urge to digress into criticism in a strong way, which allows you to stop and say, *That's not the route I am taking.*

These are just a few ideas to get you started. I want you to be on the lookout for these because they are massive opportunities to make progress quickly. Once you practice your new script, your day could be filled with challenges that you think are there to set you back. They are not.

They are there to set you up for success.

Here is where it is helpful if you have awareness of where you are most critical. Some of us are most critical of our appearance. Some are most critical of our daily eating habits. Some are most critical of our level of bravery or confidence. You know you. You know where you have the biggest hang-ups around being self-critical. And those are the areas you want to pay attention to.

If you tend to self-criticize if you overeat, you may find yourself overeating, going into a criticism cycle, and then wondering, *Why the heck did I overeat?* This is your opportunity to say, *Thanks, life, for giving me a chance to address the critic head-on.* Then, I would say, *I overate, and I will not criticize myself for that.*

If your self-criticism centers on your relationships at home, you may find that your housemates trigger you, and you berate yourself. Again, it's not ganging up on you; it's life giving you a chance to say, *I am changing my self-talk for good.*

If your criticism is directed toward others, you may find that you are overly annoyed or frustrated with others. It's a sign that you could change the critical tack and choose a new one.

If your criticism is directed toward your performance in your job, you may find yourself making a big mistake. The mistake is a sign that you have an enormous chance to talk yourself through that mistake without being critical.

The backlash has hit me, over and over, as I tried to bust free from old ideas. What helps tremendously is to see the backlash as a fortification opportunity. Life serves me the perfect situation for me to affirm what I want to be true. Life delivers me what I need to break the bonds with the critic in a concrete way. Life helps me see that I have the power, in the moment I experience the critic, to choose a different path.

Self-criticism isn't necessary, isn't helpful, and isn't natural. It's simply a habit some of us developed because we thought that was the best path for us. Now you know better.

To help you prepare for the backlash, let's revisit the exercise we did on Day Two. In this exercise, we looked for any good moment we could savor. This exercise helped us see that there are moments when we can be free of the critic. There are moments when we can feel good about ourselves. There are moments when we feel whole.

In Day Two, we not only looked for these moments, but we also used self-talk to prolong and enhance them. Let's create a list of activities that you love to do, and then add these activities to your day. Your initial work is to brainstorm a list, and I encourage you to make that list long. We are looking for activities you enjoy and that we can prolong with self-talk.

Your list will be as unique as you are. One person could list playing cards. Another could list counting yellow cars. Yet another could list watching wrestling. My list would not be helpful to you, but I'll share it anyway, so you get a flavor for what we are going for.

- Getting into a hot bath at the end of the day.
- Going on a brisk walk while I talk to myself.
- Having a good cup of coffee with full-fat cream every morning.
- Cooking dinner for people I love.
- Pulling together a great outfit from things I have in my closet.
- Getting my nails done.
- Having someone wash my hair.
- Entering a calm and relaxing room.
- Going to the spa.

- Laughing with my family.
- Writing myself notes and sending them to myself via email.
- Finding a great new TV show and enjoying it.
- Reading an awesome book.

You get the point. Make a list of activities you enjoy. Make a list of things you would do for free, even if you get paid for them. Make a list and then use it to help you coast through the backlash.

Every day for the next two weeks, pick something on your list and do it. As you do it, engage in pleasurable self-talk. What each of us deems pleasurable is a personal choice, but I personally prefer to talk to myself confidently and with great appreciation for what I am doing.

I might say, *I am so glad I made this spa appointment. I love coming here. I love how low the lighting is and how comfortable the chairs are. I am glad I am doing this for me, and I hope everyone I love takes care of themselves too.*

That's it. Just practiced appreciation to make your pleasurable activity more pleasurable.

What this does is prepare you for a life situation that you feel is a backslide. It isn't a backslide. It's an opportunity to break a bond. But I am here to tell you, I was angry over some of my backslides.

When I was building up a new idea that I wanted to grow my subscriber base for my newsletter, I found myself doubting the content and second-guessing my decision to give it away for free. I began to wonder if it was a cosmic backlash for me daring to say that I wanted more subscribers and believed in my content. It was not. It was my opportunity to double down on my belief not only in the value of my writing but also in my worthiness to have people who enjoy reading it.

When I began to practice the idea that I wanted to be motivated by love (interests, wants, and passions), I found myself devoid of wants. I felt like an empty shell. Again, I wondered whether the universe was sending me a sign to say, *You have no strong wants*. Not true. It just felt like that so I could affirm, *I want my wants to come forward*.

Here is where I will play armchair psychologist, even though I have no degree in that area: I think that our anger or frustration over the backlash helps us more powerfully stake a claim for the new idea that we are practicing. In our emotional state, we get to make a choice. And when you use the power of that emotion to make a choice for you and for your new, improved idea of life, you make big leaps ahead.

As I lost my critic, there were moments of backslide. I was preparing to speak in front of a crowd of people, and the critic came forward in such a big way that I was shaking as I spoke. It felt cosmically unfair, given all the work I had done to shake the critical thought patterns. But then I saw it for what it was: an opportunity to say that fear was not in control. I was moving forward anyway. And I gave my talk.

It was also a powerful opportunity for me to unearth limiting beliefs around my ability to speak in front of a crowd, allowing me to create new ideas to succeed.

Your work, today, is to create your list of pleasurable activities. Make it long. Then, add them into your day with self-talk. Be alert, but not fearful, of the backlash. It is a gift of an opportunity, and you will, each day, get better and better at spotting the gift and reclaiming your authority.

TAKEAWAYS

- New ideas often stir up old, contrary ideas. You are now prepared to deal with that.
- The backlash isn't a problem; it's an opportunity.
- Pleasurable activities are always a useful addition to a life well lived.

Mary is insecure in her job. She feels like she was promoted to a position that is above where she is capable. And she is sure that everyone knows that she was promoted because the company needed to show support for women. She feels like she is barely holding it all together. Her clothes are stained, her shoes are scuffed, and she can't imagine finding the time to get her nails done. She needs help to get her life together, but who has time to ask for help? She closes the door to her office because the banter she hears outside annoys her.

Mary has an attachment to a critic who believes that her value is her contribution to the office. This idea makes the critic a loud part of her life. Mary could lose the critic, and she would find the confidence of her true self.

Day 19

FIND YOUR WHY

Our work together is winding down, but I have a few more exercises that I would like to explore with you. These exercises are best done once you have done the clearing exercise from Days Sixteen and Seventeen. Your work was to empty yourself of all the reasons you have a critic, and then create a script to practice that says the opposite. Over and over, until you find yourself more at peace. Once you have done that, here are further exercises to help you clear out your limitations.

Take out a sheet of paper and write across the top, *I am ready to lose my critic*. That's your goal, which I fully support, and that's what we now want to work on. Under that want, at the top of the page, create three columns. Title the first one *Why*, the second *Intentions*, and the third *Affirmations*. With your paper prepared, let's begin.

Your work is to list every reason you can think of why you want to lose your critic, and place them in the "Why" column. Keep writing until the page is full, and then turn to the next page, make three columns, and keep going. Every idea you can come up with. Every thought that comes to mind. Every reason that motivates you to say goodbye to self-criticism.

Our work together has given you several reasons, so capture those. You might look in your notebook to refresh your recollection or to find little tidbits that you have written down as you have done these exercises. You might reread a prior section and be prompted with a reason. Or your mind may empty itself, giving you all the why statements.

Don't be choosy or judgy with your why statements. You could write, *I want to lose the critic so I can get a better job.* You could say, *I want to lose the critic because I am intrigued by the idea of a critic-less life.* You could write, *I want to lose the critic because I am convinced that criticism is not the best way to motivate.*

Your work is to think of as many reasons as you possibly can to support you in this project. If you are doing this work for your kids, say so. If you are reading this book because you are tired of the critic, write it down. If you are doing this work because you have this fundamental belief in love, then put that on the page.

Once you have several pages of reasons, it's time to process that list. Create intentions and affirmations for each why statement so that you have a go-to script when you are feeling low or like you won't succeed.

Start with the first why statement and turn it into an intention. If you wrote, *I want to experience life without the critic,* then your intention would read, *I intend to notice any time I experience life without the critic.* Or *I intend to lead a critic-free life.* Or *I will not allow the critic to affect my experience.* See what feels good to you and write out your intention.

Intentions are like rocket fuel. They help you get where you want to go faster. They aren't instantaneous or automatic, but they do help you set the stage for success. Set intentions freely, easily, and always in the direction of where you want to head.

Once you set the intention, turn it into a present-day affirmation. Using our same example, you could write, *I am critic-free.* Or *I am now living life without the critic.* Or *I am over the hump, and the critic is a thing of the past.*

Pour yourself into this project. Meaning, make the words feel like your own. Make them fun and light. Be happy as you do this work and create a worksheet that will help you advance toward a life without the critic.

If one of your why statements is around your belief in the power of love-based activities, then you would write, *I intend to go with the flow of love.* And then, *I am in the flow of love and enjoying myself every day.*

If your why statement says, *I want to be nicer to myself,* then write, *I will be nice to me.* And then affirm, *I am good and nice to myself, always.*

Keep working, filling out the worksheet until you have an intention and an affirmation for every why statement. Then—you guessed it—go practice those new statements.

This is a powerful way to find the courage to move forward with this work. We waited until today to start this work because often, our why statements are hiding behind our limiting beliefs. We first needed to clear out those limiting beliefs so we could unearth your why statements.

Why statements are your true wants. See them as the scaffolding you need to support you on a journey as big as the one we have undertaken. You want all your why statements handy to help you see that this journey is important, worthwhile, and attainable.

The why statements show us what we want, the intention gets us moving, and the affirmation takes us home.

When I do this work, I get excited. I find myself in the energy of the new place I want to be, and the energy is so palpable I can feel it. I often pull out the worksheet when I am feeling low, and by the end of a practice session, I am flying high.

Practice when it feels natural to you. I find that I practice more often at first, and then I put the worksheet away and go live. Life is not solved with one worksheet, but one worksheet can set you up for powerful success.

To help you find why statements that motivate you, I provide below a list of reasons that showcase why the critic is unnecessary, unhelpful, and not a preferred way of motivating yourself. Peruse this list and see which items on the list resonate with you. Add them to the Why column of your worksheet. And here's another tip: you can't overdo this work. For some goals, I create a new worksheet every other day, and each time I uncover more whys behind my goal. And those whys are powerful motivators.

Here are a few to consider:
- I want to experience life doing what I want rather than what I should.
- I want to find inner peace away from the critic.
- I know criticism is not a way to create sustaining results. I want sustaining results.
- The critic is an old idea, and I am ready to be done with it.
- I have no taste for fear to motivate me; I want to be motivated by doing activities I love.

- I see the power of love motivators; I want to experience more of life using love as a motivator.
- The critic has torn me down, and I am ready to build myself back up.
- The critic has taken me only so far, and I am ready to go big.
- I want more time when I feel good about myself.
- I want to enjoy life, not pick it apart.
- I want to find more to love about life.
- I want to feel comfortable in my own skin.
- I want to say kind and loving things to myself.
- I want to feel confident and self-assured.
- I want to experience life without the critic.
- I want to be calm and at peace with who I am, today.
- I want to quit striving to meet others' expectations.
- I want to set the agenda for my life.
- I am ready to let go of critical habits of thought.

Fill up your worksheet. Collect as many why statements as you can find. Process the why statements into intentions and affirmations. And then practice.

Here is why this works:

When you pull back the curtain on any goal and uncover your why statements, now you have ideas that the new goal can anchor to. By acknowledging the why statement, you activate it. Then, you pair that activated desire with an intention (here is the direction I want to head) and an affirmation (here is what it is like when I get there). These ideas are like scaffolding that you are building to support your big goal.

And losing a critic is a big goal. It's a goal you may not have had before because you didn't know you could lose the critic. It's a goal that may feel overwhelming to you once you become aware of how pervasive and pernicious a critic is. It's a goal that may seem impossible until you show up to do the work.

Your work today is the worksheet. While you do that work, congratulate yourself for coming this far. Write in your logbook, *I have turned the corner and am now building myself back up.* That's what this worksheet is. You building scaffolding for yourself to continue the work of losing the critic.

The work of getting to a critic-less life may never be done. But any movement toward a reclamation of your power is a positive movement that will pay dividends in your life. We aren't striving for perfection in that we never self-criticize. We are working toward tearing down the false beliefs that propped up the critic in the first place. And then building a fortress to keep ourselves from falling into old habits of thought.

Your worksheet, as I said, could be done, and redone, over the course of a few weeks, and you would powerfully add to your list of why statements. See any why statement as good and helpful, even if the why statement seems spiteful or vindictive. You could write, *I want to lose my critic so I can succeed and prove John wrong.* That's an OK why to write. It's a good why statement to acknowledge. And it's a valid why statement to propel you for a while.

This is where the gift of discernment comes in. Only you can decide what you allow into your life as your motivators. Personally, when I notice that I am motivated by fear (for instance, wanting to prove myself to another person or wanting to curry favor from another), I let that why statement sit there, and I ask, *Why do I want that?* I keep excavating the why until I get to the root why, which is often based on a limiting belief.

There is no judgment for why statements. There is no why statement that is off-limits. There is nothing wrong with being motivated, for a time, by wanting to prove another wrong. See it, however, for what it is: a short-term motivator anchored in fear. And you, now that you are aware of how powerful love motivators are, are ready to lose your fear motivators and pick up your love motivators.

When I find myself with why statements that make me a little uncomfortable, I do the work to excavate them further. Almost always, I find a limiting belief like this: *I need others' approval to feel good about myself.* Or *I need to look a certain way to be accepted.* Or *I have to do this to be good.* None of which is true.

We are each complex and multifaceted beings who have a host of why statements lurking under the covers of our wants. Your job is to unearth yours, process them, and use your power of discernment to find your way.

TAKEAWAYS

- Wanting to lose the critic is a worthy goal.
- Finding your why statements is a powerful exercise designed to unleash your inner spirit.
- Why statements can change over time, so redo these exercises to discover new layers to your why statements.

Shonda has an idea for a new business, but she has no capital to invest. She applies for a business loan and is turned down. She asks her parents for a loan, but they aren't sure that Shonda can make this business successful. Shonda then goes to her friends and asks for advice. She says she believes in the idea, but she needs someone else to help her get it started and show her the way. She consults with a coach, and the coach tells Shonda to table the business idea until she has saved more. Shonda leaves, dejected, and heads home.

Shonda is listening to her critic, not to her true self. Shonda could benefit from any exercise that gets her in touch with her own inner wisdom and a feeling of confidence in listening to herself.

Day 20

COMPARE TO KNOW

Your critic is a pattern of thought that you are disrupting with every exercise in this book. If you look back to where you started, in your notebook, you will see that we started with the simple premise that you could dismantle your critic. In the last section, I left you with the idea that the critic may not go away for good, and today, I want to harmonize those two ideas.

Being self-critical isn't bad, amoral, or wrong. It's just a habit. There is no harm from keeping the habit if you find that being self-critical is helpful to your life. I do not. I have found, however, that being self-aware is essential. Being self-reflective is beneficial. Being self-loving is crucial.

Self-love is a process of reclaiming all your pieces and welcoming them home. This process takes place over time. It feels, to me, like a constant recirculation of energy to love, and re-love, your past selves. One of your past selves is your critic.

There was a time when you allowed critical thoughts to dominate and bought into a belief system that you were better off if you criticized your way forward rather than loved your way forward. That was you, back then, doing the best you could with what you knew. But it was still you. And we need to love that part of you who engaged in self-criticism to break the pattern of self-criticism.

This is where some people balk. We all think that loving the parts of us who give us shame will lead to us holding onto the parts of us that give us shame. Not true. By loving all the parts of us, we can move forward in life. So you, my friend, are going to pick up your critical self and take her along for the ride.

This is what I mean when I say you can't fully be free. You can free yourself of patterns of self-criticism, but you want to collect the version of you who did the criticizing. These pieces of you are a valuable asset, and you want them for the second half of life.

The parts of you who leaned into self-criticism did so for a good reason. As I have said, the critic wants to keep us safe. That's a valid and worthy goal. That's a good thing. That's a helpful desire to carry. We welcome our desire to be kept safe, even as we untangle the idea that the way to keep us safe is to keep ourselves in line.

Those of us with a critic can be extreme rule followers. Those of us with a loud critic are often aware of whether we fit in or not. Those of us with the thought patterns of a critic are seemingly always in a mode of comparison.

That's how most of us learn. We see someone else, compare ourselves to them, and then draw conclusions. The fundamental error of the critic is that it thinks that conformance is the key to safety. The critic believes that adherence to the rules makes you safe. The critic thinks if you dot all the *I*s and cross all the *T*s, nothing bad can happen to you, which we all know is untrue.

Once the parts of you who carried the critic become aware of these false premises, you are left with a super-skill of comparison. You might think, *I am a super-noticer of other people, of societal norms, and of what it takes to fit in with this group.* You might think, *Why do I compare everything all the time?* You could feel that the critic is a natural consequence of a comparing mind.

Here is the subtle distinction I want you to consider. We all compare ourselves to others. We all seek to read the room to see how we fit in. We all come to the table with ideas of what is expected of us. The critic simply takes that good and natural tendency and then turns it into a set of rules to comply with.

To help ease the transition of welcoming back the parts of you who compare, try to fit in, or read the room, you need to practice this new idea: *comparison is how we know ourselves.* That's it. Comparison isn't bad or wrong. In fact, it can be a helpful tool to know yourself as different from the person to whom you compare yourself. Once you see this fundamental truth, then you can welcome your noticer self back into the fold to help you see how unique and special you are.

That's the missing piece you need to hear. Your comparing mind is a wonderful thing, once you redirect it toward seeing your uniqueness rather than your need to conform. Your noticing mind is wonderful for helping you retrain yourself to think differently. Your desire to fit in can be seen as a normal desire that we all carry because we see it as a path to love.

This is where a self-love practice comes in. As you apply compassion to yourself for having a critic, you welcome back your prior selves into the fold. Once back, they become powerful aspects of you who help you see where you are a unique and superlative individual who has much to offer the world.

You will, of course, continue to compare yourself to others, or compare yourself to perceived norms. The difference is that you will now use a practice of saying, *That's so interesting that I am me, and I am not like that other person.* You will see these comparisons as useful data points where you notice that you have a different preference than another person. You will welcome comparisons that help you to see and know yourself.

When I meet another who has different goals and wants, I am fascinated. I see that as evidence that my unique wants and goals make me who I am. I note the differences between us, and I no longer think, *I wonder if I should be like that.* Or *I wonder if I should try that.* Or *I wonder if I need to do that to succeed.*

Instead, I have found comfort in seeing others, noticing others, and comparing myself to others, not as a measure of either of us, but as a confirmation of my individual wants and needs.

I see wants and desires as emanating from my soul, so each time I can capture a unique aspect of me, I write it down. Each time I find a nugget about myself by comparing myself with another, I make a note. Each time I notice that someone else has something I admire, I collect a want.

Your skills at noticing, comparing, and judging can be put to good use, if you work on it. Even judging can serve a purpose. When I see someone who is conducting their life in a way that I do not prefer (and head into judgment), I now stop myself and say, *I am so glad that I am me and that I have a different preference for how I want to live.* I don't need to stew in judgment or even assign any emotion to the conclusion; I simply need to use my skills to know myself.

As I have written, those of us with a strong critic often shy away from self-reflection because we fear the backlash of the critic. Now is the time to lean into a project of getting to know and love yourself, based on your differences from other people.

Here is one way to approach that. You have a noticing and comparing mind. Celebrate that. Say, *I am so glad that I am good at noticing details and seeing how I am different from others. I am going to use this skill to collect data on myself.*

When your noticing mind draws your attention over and over to one person, sit and ask yourself, *What want is this showing me?* Often, we find ourselves drawn to people who have something we want. Note your want.

When your comparing mind serves you an idea that you are different from another person, welcome that difference not as a shortcoming but as a facet of what makes you unique. Write down what makes you special or unique.

When your judging mind comes forward and serves you up a conclusion, use that conclusion to say, *Here is what I want from life.*

This is a new task for your mind. You may have previously used all these skills (noticing, comparing, and judging) as fodder for the critic. No more. Now you are using these skills to create a composite sketch of who you truly are.

I would start with preferences and work my way up to passions.

When I notice that I have a different preference from another, I say, *Here is what I prefer.* If you want to make this more fun, write it down. When I notice that my natural inclinations are different from others, I double down and say, here is a preference that makes me unique. When I notice I have a strong preference for a particular direction with life, I note it as a want.

Wants are the language of the soul, so a project to capture your wants is a project to nurture. It is a project to help you collect, see, and love all your parts, as a way of practicing self-love. We only know ourselves, truly, through what we want, so see all the wants you are capturing as tiny parts of you that you are welcoming back home.

As you collect your wants, some will rise to the top. Some will become more urgent. Some will become your next passion project, calling you forward each day. That's when you will know you have truly broken free of the critical mindset; you'll work on projects for the pure joy of doing them.

Your comparing mind is an asset if you can break the habit of moving from comparison to criticism. Which you can. It's a matter of redirecting this important asset to a collection of data about you—your wants and desires.

Every comparison holds an opportunity for you to say, *I want*. Every judgment holds an opportunity for you to pause and notice what you want. Every outward reflection your mind wanders to is a chance to celebrate your unique differences from the rest of the world.

The art of holding a want is an art to practice. The beauty of every want is that it reveals a little of you *to* you. See the collection you are making as an amalgamation of your innate desires, which are as close to a soul blueprint as one can find.

TAKEAWAYS

- Your mind is one of your best assets; put it to work for you.
- Comparisons help you know yourself better; thank any person you compare yourself to.
- Judgments help us know our wants. Surrender the judgment and find the want.

Carlos can't sit still. He learns best when moving around, and that hasn't changed as he has aged. Luckily, he has a job that allows him to be on his feet, moving and staying active most of the day. Carlos looks with admiration at the people who work in an office and knows that his own path was cut off by his inability to finish a book, take tests, or complete a project. He tells his children that they won't be the same as him, and he makes sure that they are always on top of their homework and school projects. Carlos hopes that one day his children get to work in an office, like he has always wanted.

Carlos's critic may have been created when he was younger and led him to believe that his active spirit was a problem to be solved instead of a characteristic to celebrate. Carlos would benefit if he dealt with these old messages and found a way to love himself as he is. His kids would benefit too.

Day 21

NOTICE IN NEUTRAL

Yesterday, we began a process to reclaim our power of noticing, comparing, and judging. These are skills that you have on high alert when you are living with a critic. We used those skills and turned them on their head to help you see that those skills are useful to know who you are.

They are also useful to see what you think.

When you are a powerful noticer, which you are if you had a critic, then you can use that skill to notice your thoughts. You can, as soon as today, affirm that you are using your skill of noticing to help you know your mind.

We can't change our thinking until we see our thinking. And your skill at noticing will help you see your own beliefs.

Beliefs are like cookie cutters. What you believe affects the shape of what you get from life. If your beliefs are broad, expansive, and inclusive, then that's your experience. If your beliefs are tight, rigid, and divisive, then that's your experience. All of us have a mixture of beliefs, and your goal is to improve your beliefs to help you succeed.

Beliefs are neutral. There aren't good ones or bad ones. To me, there are only helpful and more helpful beliefs. That's how I like to see them. They are all helping me. And some I reframe so they are more helpful to me. To do that, I begin with noticing.

Noticing, like beliefs, is also neutral. When you notice, you don't move into judgment or any sort of conclusion. You just notice. You practice simply observing what you are thinking and might even, say, *Well, that's so interesting that I am thinking that.* Noticing is done as a dispassionate observer who has no dog in the fight. Noticing is like ice-skating without any friction. You just smoothly pass over the thoughts.

I am using visuals to convey a feeling. Noticing feels open and loose. Judging feels tight and narrow. And you want to aim for open and loose.

Your meditation practice will set you up for success. If you practiced going within and breathing, even for one minute, you are developing a habit of noticing. That's all meditation is. Thoughts come up and you do your best to simply see them, without attaching to them. You can do this aware or unaware. Meaning, you can notice a thought and see it pass by, or you can simply breathe and be aware that you are breathing. In either case, I have had success in letting go.

As you slow down to allow and merely notice, you will have more awareness of your thinking. You'll enter a room and notice that you see one person before anyone else, and you'll realize that your mind is saying, *I want to sit by her.* Or you will walk into the grocery store and find yourself pulled toward an item and notice that your mind says, *This sounds good to me.* Or you will feel yourself pulled to move or stand up, and you'll notice that your thought is *I want to move.*

Many of us with a critic stay busy to avoid the critic. Your next project is to enter a period of purposeful slowing down to notice your thinking. It's not a forever thing; it's just a respite to allow your skill of noticing to be used to see your thinking mind.

The thinking mind is busy with all sorts of ideas. When you purposefully slow down, if only for a minute, you stop the mind from racing off, and you regain a little power. When you do this with an intention to notice what you are thinking, then you have a powerful tool to see your own beliefs.

Your thoughts aren't a problem or even a deterrent. They are useful information as to where you are today. At any given moment of time, you are a mixture of your wants, your fears, and your beliefs. What we want to do is notice where you are today.

Beliefs affect our every waking moment, so they are simply part of life. Your work is to notice when you carry a belief that is not serving you. And noticing occurs once you slow down.

Slowing down could be as simple as sitting quietly for ten minutes and breathing. Slowing down could be a walk where you simply observe yourself. Slowing down, for me, involves writing so I can use that process to see what I am thinking. The more you practice, the better you get at noticing your own thoughts.

We've done this with the clearing exercises that we practiced in prior sections. That was an exercise to pull out our blocks so we could address them. You'll want to do the same with your beliefs so you can alter them to help you succeed.

Noticing beliefs is something I prefer to do over time. I prefer to allow life to deliver me experiences that help me see my beliefs so I can change my beliefs. When I notice that I am feeling tense or anxious, I ask myself, *What am I thinking?* I let those thoughts come forward and simply notice them. Often, those thoughts are limiting or self-defeating, and I make a choice to think differently. But I can only get to the new, improved thought when I notice.

A practice of noticing, in neutrality, serves several purposes. As I said, it helps you see your thoughts. It also helps you disconnect from blame, shame, and guilt. If your observation is neutral, there is no reason to move into judgment. The thought or situation simply *is* and needs no critical assessment. Last, it helps you break free from the critic on a deeper level as noticing becomes sufficient for your purposes.

As we have learned, the critic is based on fundamental misunderstandings. One is that you need to make a critical assessment of each situation. Not true. You can practice the art of noticing neutrally and see that a critical assessment of anyone or anything is optional.

Critical assessments are based on fear. When you enter a room and think, *I have to figure out my place here*, you operate in fear. When you enter a new situation and think, *I must make sure I am safe here*, you proceed in fear. When you encounter a new idea and think, *I must make sense of this*, you are in fear. What you want to move to is neutrality.

As you go about your day, practice seeing each segment with neutrality. See yourself as a neutral observer of life and the new situation, and simply observe. I do this with self-talk. You could walk into a room and think, *There is one open seat. I will take that seat.* You could walk into a store and say, *I am here to find shoes, and I see the shoes over there.* You could go into your car and say, *I am ready to drive home, and the commute is flowing well.*

This deliberate self-talk slows down the brain and allows you to enter a less critical frame of mind. Your goal is to keep your observations neutral. To simply enter a segment of your day and name and notice neutrally.

A critical assessment is usually done on autopilot. A neutral assessment habit will take time to develop. See yourself on a journey where you have neutral noticing skills today, which will become better skills tomorrow. This neutral noticing will become second nature, but you will first need to practice.

A few ways to practice are:
- Take yourself on a walk and simply walk and talk, whatever comes to mind. Get used to the idea that your thoughts are there for you and that by speaking them, they become more tangible and less like background noise. Remember, the critic runs on autopilot for most of us.
- Make lists of what you are thinking when you have uncertainty or a big decision in front of you. Just sit with a pen and paper and write your concerns, what you know, and what you don't know.
- When you have free time, such as when waiting or in traffic or commuting, make a game out of noticing. List what you see around you without attaching any judgment to it. Just say, *I see a tree, a yellow car, a man walking.* This is a great way to retrain the mind to notice in neutral.
- If you enjoy working out, do your workout with a sense of awareness of how you feel and what you think. You might say, *I feel so strong as I lift this.* Or *I am getting better at this.* Just let the thoughts come to you, but give them voice.

- If you have a daily habit, set an intent to combine it with neutral noticing. If you make a cup of coffee every day, bring a sense of awareness to each step, in neutral. If you make your bed, do so with a running dialogue of what you are doing.

Those of us with loud critics are accustomed to a cacophony of noise in our back brain that just sorta exists. This process stops the incessant chatter in its tracks and forces you to convert those amorphous thoughts into words. Where you can better handle them. The point is not to censor yourself; in fact, the point is to say what you think. Once you out your critical thinking, it often abates in your experience, or you can talk back to it to say what you believe.

Noticing in neutral is your new work. Write yourself a note, pin it to the top of your notes app, or make these words visible: *I can notice in neutral.* Or *I am choosing to practice noticing in neutral.* Or *I am ready to take control of the background noise and will do so by noticing in neutral.*

TAKEAWAYS

- You can develop a habit of noticing in neutral and reveal more of yourself to you.
- Most situations benefit from a practice of moving them into neutral.
- You have the power to notice in neutral; use it to benefit you.

Martha thought she knew how to assemble the furniture, but she finds herself sitting amid a bunch of scattered pieces, several screws, and instructions that look like they were made by aliens trying to communicate nonverbally. She sighs as she pulls herself up from the floor and remembers that her husband told her this wasn't a good idea. Her dander up, she fights back with a thought, *I won't let him see me fail*. She forces herself back down and works, angry the whole time, until she has the furniture assembled. She feels no joy from this but is only angry over the whole process.

Martha's critic seems to think that what others think of her pertains to her. Her better course? Listen to her own guidance and do whatever she wants.

Day 22

SAYING *I WANT*

Your wants are a clue to your best life, so let's do the work of coaxing them forward.

As I said, if you have a critic, you might have a habit of want suppression. You could be someone who does what is expected and who is unaccustomed to listening to and following your wants. You could, in fact, be so out of touch that you think you don't have wants of your own.

Not true. You're just out of practice. And today we get back up on the horse, welcoming your wants.

We all understand the horse metaphor. You get kicked off, and you make a choice to get back on. What I want you to take from that is this: you always have a choice to welcome your wants back.

You don't age out of your wants, as best I can tell. Nor do you lose your wants. They just sit patiently on the sidelines until you allow them back into your life. Like old friends who you haven't talked to in a while, your wants will result in a sweet reunion. But first you must create new habits of allowing wants to live.

When a person engages in want repression, what happens is that they notice a want, and then part of their brain says, *We can't have that*. Or *That want is improper*. Or *That want is too big*. And then they feel uncomfortable, and they associate wanting with discomfort. It's not the want that hurts; it's the soul-crushing denial of your want that hurts.

We will learn to have a want without trying to figure out how we get what we want. That's the headline: you can have a want and make no movement toward satisfying it. You can greet a want and hold it perfectly, without rushing ahead to determine your next steps. You can bravely and boldly say, *I want*, and let that be enough.

To do this, we create a new habit of saying *I want*, to make it a repeatable function in our life but also to neutralize wants. Remember, wants are never a problem. They are simply an expression of your best path forward.

As you go about your day, practice saying *I want* in each situation where you find yourself. You could tie this to your new habit of noticing. You could enter a room, notice in neutral, and then think, *I want*. As in *I want this meeting to go smoothly*. Or *I want everyone to get along at lunch*. Or *I want them to listen to me and what I have to say*. The want doesn't matter. What matters is that you acknowledge it.

We all have wants. We all have something we are trying to get. We all have a reason for being where we are. Your job, and only job, is to notice your wants.

By noticing wants throughout the day, you will see that wants aren't anything to fret over or to get disappointed about. They are simply a part of life. Of course you have wants; you are a living, breathing human. You could have a limiting belief that your wants are improper. You could have a block that says wants are vain or greedy. You could be telling yourself it's better not to want than to want. Those are all just ideas keeping you from your wants.

Wants are directional signs showing you where to go next. Where to spend your time. What's the next best step for you. They are useful and helpful to keep you on your path. They can be as simple as *I want to take a break*, or as big as *I want to write a book*. No matter the want, note it.

When I first began to cultivate this habit, I wrote down the want. That process helped me better articulate and see the want. It also helped me from going into fix-it mode, where I try to figure out a way to satisfy the want. I would write it down, look at it, and say, *Yep, that's what I want.*

Honesty is your best policy here. It's only you talking to you, so no reason to censor yourself. If you want someone to leave you alone, say so, if only in your head. If you want to create a rift with another, own it, and let it be until you are ready to process that. If you want to tell someone off, say so, even if you keep quiet.

Wants do not need to be acted on. That's the message you need to hear. And wants are not the source of your pain; blocking your wants is.

Practicing saying *I want* is also a shortcut to stop the critic. Often, we cruise through life in autopilot mode, which is where the critic lives. When you make a deliberate intention to bring your awareness to your wants, you silence the critic, if only for a moment, and regain your sense of power.

Saying *I want* can be fun. It's you talking to you, collecting wants all day. It's you talking to you, making a claim for your authentic self.

It's been a while since we talked about the true you, so here's a reminder. She's the you on the inside. She's the part of you who is always loving, always available, and always pursuing what you want. What gets us hung up is that many of us think that "being loving" means we are pushovers; we think it means we quash our own wants in favor of others and are nice all the time. Not true. Being loving means that, first and foremost, you love yourself. And you do that by acknowledging your wants.

Wants need not be flashy or over-the-top unless that's fun for you. I might go through a day where all I say is, *I want a break, I want to feel good, and I want to be at peace with this situation*. Other days, I give it more color and say, *I want to experience laughter today, I want to be surprised by life, or I want to get a lot done today*. Still other days, I am on fire with wants and listing them everywhere I go.

When my mind wanders into how to get what I want, I like to tell it, *The hows are not my concern right now. I am only focused on the wants.* Hows are the bane of existence for the critic. The critic always wants to know the how. *How will we get this? How will this event go? How will I know we are safe in this situation?* The more you can divorce yourself from the hows, the more you can divorce yourself from the critic.

To take this one step further, create a master list of wants that you add to every day. You could list out every major category of your life and then write an *I want* statement for each. Here is a list of categories:
- Homelife
- Career
- Finances
- Personal development
- Relationships

- Spirituality
- Goals
- Physical health
- Life experiences
- Aging
- Mental health
- Fitness
- Hobbies
- Home organization

That is just a sampling. With each one, you could craft an *I want* statement. You could write, *I want a clean and organized home. I want work that fulfills me. I want hobbies that inspire me. I want a healthy relationship with my daughter. I want to age with good health.* Just go down the line and say what you want.

Wants that inspire us are called goals, and I have lots of those. But I also have wants that I allow to live by acknowledging them, even if I see no way that they will come true for me. I might say, *I want all my children to live under my roof,* even though my oldest is now away at school, and I know that is best for her. I don't try to quash the want; I honor it.

Wants have this curious ability to bring us back to life. We have all experienced this, when you stumble into an interest or a curiosity, and it calls you forward until you satisfy your desire. When a person is in touch with wants, we use words like "full of life" or "lit from within." These all signify that those who want more are accessing more life force when they do.

Your project of leaning into your wants has an excellent side benefit: you know yourself better. You notice your preferences, your desires, and your passions. You see that your wants are what make you unique, and that uniqueness is to be celebrated. The more you gain clarity on your wants, the more you gain clarity in life. Nearly every moment of indecision or confusion I experience can be tied to not being clear on what I wanted. When I sit and gain that clarity, I can hold on to a want, even if it doesn't come to fruition.

Learning not to judge your wants takes time, so just roll with it until you get into a habit of saying *I want*. In fact, make it a point to air out the wants you are embarrassed of, think are wrong, or feel uncomfortable with. They don't help you if you let them fester in the background, held back by your web of mistaken beliefs. When you air them out, you often gain freedom from them and can move about life in a lighter and freer way.

Your wants are there, under all the rubble of your fears and mistaken beliefs. Let them come forward to enliven your experience, to call you forward in life, and to show you the true you.

TAKEAWAYS

- Your wants are valuable assets; collect them and keep them.
- You can articulate a want for every area of your life; go broad at first.
- Saying *I want* is a habit that is useful for every area of your life.

Anton can't wait to get home. The big game is tonight, and he is pumped to see his team in the finals. He has been thinking of the game all day, and every time he does, it brings a smile to his face. He loves sports. Upon pulling into the driveway, he knows there is a problem. The kids' toys are everywhere, and there is clearly evidence of a paint spill on the driveway. Anton exits his car to find his wife at her wits' end and offering him the baby in her arms. Anton takes the child and tries to ask what happened but is shut down by his wife. She gets into the car and drives away, leaving Anton speechless. He shrugs and heads into the house, ordering pizza for dinner and inviting the kids to join him as he watches the game.

Anton seems to have a healthy relationship with his critic and seems to possess a natural connection to his true self.

Day 23

EMOTIONS

Your new habit of saying *I want* is taking root and is now part of your everyday experience. You wake up and seize the day as the person in charge. You enter a room and make it a point to notice and to say *I want*. And you are creating a collection of wants that are revealing the true you to you.

Be nice to yourself. If you are, for the first time, claiming your want to succeed, you could feel scared and alone as you do that. If you are, for the first time, welcoming in the wants you had as a child, you could be feeling vulnerable and full of shame. If you are doing this work, then you are likely feeling many feelings that you didn't expect from the process of reclaiming yourself.

Emotions are a part of life. They aren't good. They aren't bad. They simply are. They can, if you allow them, become useful and helpful to a life well lived, but you may first need to drop your habit of emotional suppression.

The critic takes aim at your conduct, and a common target I have seen is a person's emotional state. If we get angry, the critic says, *You're not supposed to be angry.* If you get sad, the critic says, *What did you do to make us sad?* If you get frustrated, the critic leaps in and says, *What did you do wrong here?* That's a typical pattern for the critic because the critic thinks that if we have no emotions, then we are safe.

Emotions can feel like they are carrying us away. They aren't, but their power can be great. Let's use that power to our advantage.

First, you may need to welcome in your emotions. You could need inner dialogue to help you resee emotions as helpful. You could need time to allow yourself to feel your emotions again.

Here is where I am going to strongly suggest that you find a trusted therapist or clergy to meet with if you feel you have no emotions. The work I am offering is for those of us who express our emotions but who also have hang-ups around the propriety of anger or frustration or even hatred. We feel our emotions but have certain ones we don't give into. If you, however, are feeling devoid of emotions, please get help.

Emotions that I welcome in are happiness, satisfaction, and excitement. Emotions that I try to avoid are frustration, disappointment, and fear. The former feel good, and the latter feel less good. And that's how I think it's supposed to work.

When I feel good, I feel more closely aligned with my true essence. I feel like I am unstoppable. I feel like there is good in me and in the world. So I lean into those emotions and do my best to savor them.

I also, however, use my negative emotions to help me as well.

When I experience a negative emotion, it's a signal to me that I have cleanup work to do. Something in me is circling on an unhelpful idea, perseverating on a story that doesn't benefit me, or creating new stories that weigh me down. And each of those is an opportunity to clear out a limiting belief and replace it with a more helpful belief.

To get to a place of allowing in your negative emotions, you might need new ideas. Bring out your notebook and write these down:

- Emotions are helpful indicators of what I am thinking.
- Emotions help me see where I have the greatest opportunity for change.
- Emotions, of all types, are welcomed by me.

As I mentioned in the chapter on the backlash, don't be surprised if, after you welcome in your emotions, you find yourself in an emotionally charged situation, and you get to decide whether you will welcome in your emotions, or whether you will revert to old patterns and suppress them. My advice: prepare yourself now to be ready for a few supercharged emotions, and when they arrive, say, *I am so glad you are here to help me level up my life.*

For example, you could find yourself driving and be so frustrated with other drivers that you want to scream. Scream! Let it out. Tell them all what you think, in the privacy of your own car. Get it off your mind. Then, affirm, *These emotions are helping me, even if I can't yet see how.*

You may also find yourself sad. Sobbing. Feeling an overwhelming void over a loved one who passed years ago. Again, let that emotion come in; be present for it and express it. Emotions always pass through more quickly once you express them. Always.

You could, as well, find yourself in a life situation that makes you so angry that you feel volatile. Lean into it. Say how you feel. Let that anger be a clean sweep through you, helping you clear out all the ideas that said, *Anger is a bad thing.*

I want to touch on anger further, as many of us with a critic have issues with anger. Here is what helped me: realizing that anger is better than depression. I would rather see my loved ones angry than depressed. I would rather feel the white-hot rage of anger than to feel nothing at all. I would rather use my anger to move through a disappointing situation quickly and easily, instead of repressing it and causing it to build up in me.

So I made peace with anger and began allowing it in.

Your emotions are all there for you, waiting to be expressed. Mine came back to me in waves, and as long as I stayed present and let them be whatever they were, I found myself moving through them quickly. In fact, I learned to enjoy the anger. I learned to see extreme frustration as a huge opportunity. I began to see sadness as evidence that I had loved.

Your efforts to welcome in your emotions will help you see that emotions can be an important part of a process of losing your critic.

As you develop a habit of noticing and expressing your emotions, you avoid a morass of background thinking that we all do when we haven't expressed ourselves. When our emotions simmer on the back burner, they just become a confused mess. The easiest and fastest way out of that background thinking—which is where the critic lives—is to express your emotions.

You don't need to tell people off, or even confront every enemy. You only need to be honest with yourself about how you are feeling.

If a child is disappointing you, own that, even as you hold an intent to help them succeed.

If your job is boring, say so, even as you continue to work it to support your family.

If your life is not what you want it to be, pour out all your feelings, and let them be a catalyst of sorts for you to resee.

Emotional processing isn't just a mental health activity. I see it as a core spiritual practice. To be open, if only in my prayers, as to what is getting on my nerves, what has me scared, and what has me feeling low. There, I can be honest, open, and real with exactly how I feel, whereas society makes it hard for us to own our baser feelings.

Once you develop a habit of emotional expression, you'll soon see that your strongest emotions are giving you a clue of where you need to go next. If you are feeling frustrated day in and day out, that frustration holds clues as to where you could change your thinking. If you are angry for a long period of time, that anger shows you that you are applying a standard to others or yourself that is unrealistic. And if you are sad for many days in a row, you could benefit from exploring that sadness and letting it air out.

Here is where the critic may flare. Again, the critic thinks that strong emotions indicate a screwup. Not true. Strong emotions indicate the area where your attention is needed the most. That's it. See it as an early warning signal from your own spirit, helping you to tend to yourself.

That's all we are doing: our best job tending to ourselves. The work of healing up your patterns of criticism is good and worthy work that helps you present as a healed human being to the world. What would our world be like if we all took one step toward healing? What would our world feel like if we all allowed our emotions to express, to pass, and to move on? What could you accomplish if you knew your emotions were an indication of your best path forward?

These questions are what drove me to write this book. I sensed that all of us, on some level, are self-critical and could benefit from even a 1 percent improvement in that cycle. If you did nothing else other than allow your emotions to be whatever they are, you'd be on an upward trajectory. If you did nothing but read this book, without doing any exercises, you still would benefit. If you set one intention to lose your critic, you'd be on your way toward loosening the critic's hold.

Your emotions are gifts if you can get to a place of simply witnessing them, accepting them, and using them. With a practice of expression, done honestly, you free yourself of the hold that emotions have on you. And then, with that habit of expression, you can ask yourself, *What was I thinking when I had that emotion?*

Emotions are harbingers of our internal dialogue. If you allow your mind to chatter and spin tales, you may find that your emotions control you. Take a step toward control of that chatter, and the critic, by owning your emotions, naming your emotions, and expressing your emotions.

TAKEAWAYS

- All emotions are helpful.
- Emotions are neutral, and we judge them based on how we feel.
- Use your emotions to discover what you are thinking.

Carol never takes a break. She feels like her work is more important than any other aspect of her life, so she puts in the hours, brings her work home with her, and self-identifies as an overachiever. She regularly misses dinner with her family and isn't home when she says she will be. She has confidence, charisma, and self-drive, and sees herself as outside of the realm of spirituality, which she sees as too woo-woo for her taste. Plus, she has stuff to accomplish, and spirituality seems like a speed bump in life.

Carol's critic has convinced her that her value is in her work, and Carol would benefit if she challenged that assumption. She might find that her joy in life would return if she found a way to divorce herself from the critic who is driving her to work rather than to do things that she enjoys.

Day 24

OPEN YOUR HEART

Your work, if you allow it, is to stay open and aware as you go about your day, which is the opposite of life with the critic.

The critic, running in the background, pumps out messages that say, *Watch out, you should do this, and you aren't good enough.* Those messages become a soundtrack for your day if you tune in to the critic. By staying open and aware, you tune out the critic and tune in to the true you.

Life is not an all-or-nothing affair. It's a continuum of experiences, each one bringing us closer to who we truly are. When you hold an intent to remain open and aware most of the time, you see that life seems to swirl around you, but you remain unaffected. This state of being, which feels like a good exhalation to me, is the state I strive for most of the day.

I don't always achieve it, nor am I looking for perfection. Instead, I am looking for moments throughout my day when I exhale, set an intent to open my heart, and then allow. These moments of respite from the critic are just what you need to jump-start your breakup.

I see openness as an extension of a meditation. It's where I sit, even if I am doing something else, and set an intent to be and remain open. To remain aware of the stray critical thought. To remain conscious of where my mind takes me. I don't do this all day, but I do endeavor to use moments of respite to my best advantage.

Openness isn't hard once you allow it. It's just a way of saying, *I can't control everything going on around me, so instead I will sit here, openly, and allow life to be what it is.*

This work is directly contrary to the critic, who often feels a need to control life. Who believes that you will be OK if everyone around you is OK. Who causes you to think that you must control your experience to have a good life.

Now that I am on the other side of life with the critic, I can tell you that the far more empowering way to live is to adopt an attitude of excited nonchalance about what life is serving you. By this I mean, I am excited as I have a positive expectation of good things coming my way, but I don't get bound up in the details of what or how. I simply do my best to stay open and see what comes.

Life with the critic causes you to close. So let's practice being open.

To do this, set aside a few minutes to be alone. Sit in a comfortable spot and simply breathe. Set an intention to stay open the whole time you are in this position. Just breathe. See what you notice.

When I do this, I notice that my field of awareness expands. I notice that my breathing deepens and slows. I notice that I feel all syrupy and languid as I sit. Once my sit is over, I return to my day.

Throughout my day, I look for opportunities to practice being open. I might write, as I am right now, and allow myself to stay open for maximum effect. I might sit through a meeting and stay open as I listen to others speak or present. I drive and try to stay open as I relax into an easy commute. There are many opportunities to pause and say, *I am going to simply stay open.*

Staying open, to me, is the antithesis of critic mode. It's a conscious decision, by me, to tune in to myself. It's a natural process that most of us forgot as we grew up and began to fear.

When I express an intent to stay open, for even a few minutes, I seem to find a peace inside that supports me through situations where it is harder to stay open. Stressful situations that life serves up, that many of us feel like we can't avoid. Even those situations benefit if I can find one minute, in the thick of the stress, to be open.

I now do this as a matter of habit. I find a place where I am sitting still, express an intent to be open, and then just breathe into the void. That's how it feels to me because it's this space where there is no internal chatter, judgment, or comparison. Just awareness.

To do this work, you'll only need to remember that you plan to try to stay open. That's the hardest part. Remembering. To facilitate this, take out your phone and set up a recurring reminder that goes off every two hours that simply says, *Stay open.* Even in a meeting, you could glance at the alert on your phone, decide to stay open, and relax. I see waiting in line as a chance to practice. Or waiting to pick up one of my kids. You can easily find time to stay open.

This work is the equivalent of detachment to me. It says, *I am OK exactly as I am, and I can detach from any judgment of myself.* It also helps me to accept life as it is today and stop resisting life based on what I think it should be. People disappoint me, life serves up tough scenarios, and the world can seem crazy, but I can, for a moment, decide to stay open.

This practice helps me stop the critic in its tracks and gives me a tremendous sense of peace. I feel like the world is OK, even if only for a moment. I feel like I am OK in that moment. I feel like anything is possible in that moment.

Openness, to me, is synonymous with miracles. It's a way of sitting and saying, *I am here for the miracles, and I know my best path, at times, is to simply get out of the way*, which means to get out of my head and into my heart space while I stay open.

Your work, if you choose it, is to holding an intent to stay open. Don't worry that you don't know exactly what it means to be open; just try it as a way of effective detachment from the critic.

TAKEAWAYS

- One way to approach life is to try to stay open; it benefits me greatly to do so.
- Staying open is about intention; set an intent to stay open.
- Staying open feels broad and expansive.

Roger has no idea what to do with his life. He is searching in bookstores, online, and anywhere he can think of to find his purpose. He feels destined for more but can't picture what that is. He keeps seeking outside himself, looking for a sign of what he should do with his life. He knows there are many people who need help, but Roger does not feel inspired to do service work. He just wishes that someone would show up and tell him what to do, and then, he thinks, he would be OK.

Roger has a critic who is external to him, which has caused him to lose confidence in himself and his own inner guidance. Roger would benefit from going within and seeking the answers for himself as to his best course forward, rather than relying on other people to shape his future. His critic will go silent as he goes within.

Day 25

DAYDREAMS AS TOOLS

By now your notebooks are getting full. You are collecting new ideas, words to practice, and lists that make you happy. You are logging your days and noting the positive things that you accomplish. You are creating new habits of noticing, and those habits are helping you find more good moments to log, to journal about, and to experience.

One trait I have noticed about those of us in the critic category is that we don't see ourselves as creative. We often see ourselves as more "law-and-order" type people, or perhaps even as "rule followers." We aren't typically open-minded and often have fixed ideas about how the world works. Not all of us, but some of us.

If you fall into the category where you say you are more analytical than creative, then this next exercise will help you open your mind so the critic can go away. That's how I visualize it. Me, with my own mind, creating an escape hatch where I let my critic out of my experience.

The critic is, at its base, a fear. It could be a fear that you aren't good enough, or a fear that you must prove yourself worthy. It could even be a fear that you need to act a certain way to be loved, respected, or valued. Whatever the fear, it is the anchor point of the critic. And your best path forward is to figure out a way to carve out that fear from your life.

To do this, we engage in a creative exercise where you write down everything you did for one entire day. The cereal you had for breakfast. The sneakers you wore to work. The lunch you had at the bistro. The walk you took outside. The car you almost hit in the garage. The sass you got from your teenager. The befuddlement you felt with your phone. The garbage you took to the curb. The sheets you felt when you crawled into bed. Just write it out, storylike, and put in as many details as you remember. This is your analytical brain at its finest, collecting and remembering details.

Now, take that story and rewrite it so that every event of the day went your way. If you struggled to decide what shoes to wear, write how the decision was easy, obvious, and made you happy. If your teenager sassed, write a story of how she was inquisitive and open-minded when you chatted. If you felt low or undervalued at work, tell a tale of how you were valued and appreciated. Just keep writing until you better each event of the day, showing it going your way.

This is daydreaming, and you probably think you aren't good at it. Here is why. Those of us with a critic often see daydreaming as a "waste of time" or even "making things up," which the critic deems bad. The critic also wants to figure out the hows of everything, so it gets busy planning out the route, even when you are still in the daydreaming phase. This rush to the hows stops the daydreaming in its tracks and causes you to shut off your imagination.

One of the side effects of a strong critic is that you stop imagining a better future, and you only plan for a better future. The difference between those two actions is where possibility lies. One makes you open to new possibilities; the other tends to cut you off. And you want to stay open to new possibilities.

Daydreaming is one way to open yourself to new possibilities, but it doesn't work well if you think you aren't good at it. Hence, your exercise in rewriting your day.

All of us can take a concrete situation and improve it. All of us can see how a situation that was negative can be turned into a situation that is positive, or even neutral. All of us can tell a story of a better day than the one we had.

Now use your rewrite of your day to take one more turn of the daydream. This time you will rewrite your story again, and this time, make it as over-the-top as you can. If you wrote of a day when the traffic was easy, now you write of a day when you were chauffeured to work in a private car. Or you were outfitted with a jet pack and flew there. Or you took a bullet train and arrived refreshed. Write whatever comes to mind, but do your best to supersize your daydream as much as possible.

Your new supersized daydream is now a fun way to envision your life. If you are feeling low, spend time with your daydream and let it cheer you up or make you smile. Try to visualize all the ways you could make your day easier, more fun, or more productive. Whatever floats your boat.

A supersized daydream is usually out of reach of the critic. The critic sees it as so over-the-top that it doesn't bother you with the hows.

The critic looks at the fantasy you created and says, *That's just a wild fantasy.* And it is, but it holds important information. About you.

What we daydream about is a wonderful indicator of what we want from life. As you now know, your wants are important parts of you to collect. Wants are the lifeblood of a life well lived, so harvest your wants from your fantastical daydream.

To do this, sit with the daydream and ask yourself, *What does this show me?* If you wrote a fantasy where you got the day off work and were teleported to the beach, you could note, *I want to take more time off from work, and I want to spend more time on the beach.* If you wrote a tale of a person getting huge accolades for a new discovery, then you could note, *I want to be seen, heard, and appreciated for my work.* If you wrote a daydream that had you winning the lottery, then you could note that you want to enhance your finances.

All of these are wants that are worthy of your attention. Here is why: you had to sneak them by the critic to out them.

When you find a way to bypass the critic, use it to help you see where you might be repressing a want. As we noted earlier, the critic often causes you to ignore your wants because the critic has deemed them impossible or invalid or wrong. You will use your fantasy daydream as an end run around the critic, and then you can capture your wants.

When I do this, I always uncover wants that I wasn't totally owning. When I write a daydream of having someone do my hair every day in my home, I can own that I want an easy hairstyle that looks good, which the critic might dismiss as vain or superficial. When I write of a giant house with bedrooms for guests, I can say, with certainty, that I want to create space for guests in my home. When I write of a future where everyone is self-aware and full of love, I know I have a true desire to help make the world a better place.

The critic doesn't like daydreams. The critic likes rules and judgments. See this exercise as a practice of purposefully running away from the critic to go spend time in the other hemisphere of your brain. The creative side.

The creative side is where we find solutions, possibilities, and new ideas. All of which add to the enjoyment of life. The analytical side often sees problems, lack, and certainty, which may be a place to be, but it's not a place that you want to live most of the time.

The process of losing your critic is enhanced once you daydream on the regular. For every major area of your life, you could create a script of how you want things to go, and then you could supersize it to see where you have unacknowledged wants. You could create a script for a day at work, a day with your family, and a day with your friends. You could create a script for your love life, your social life, and your home life. You could create a script for your finances, your health, and your physical fitness. All of it would reveal your wants.

Before we can achieve what we want, we have to know what we want. If you have been denying your wants, or operating life based on fear, you may have lost touch with your true wants. This exercise is a great way to reestablish a connection with the true you and ferret out your wants.

What this exercise also does is open your creative mind. You are creative; you just have lived more of life on the analytical side of the aisle. And the more you lean into your creative side, the more fun you have in life.

That's how I see it. Life is a balance. But when I am all work and no play, I lose my edge. I become tense. I become overly emotional. I become out of balance. Leaning into my creativity helps me welcome that playful energy, which is where I like to spend time now that I see myself as a daydreamer.

Over-the-top daydreams help free me of the critic, if only for the ten minutes that I am having fun. These sessions, over time, add up to a more and more weakened connection with the critic, which over time becomes a once-in-a-while encounter instead of an everyday encounter.

Your work throughout this book has been difficult at times. This one exercise should be fun and lighthearted. Embrace it as an activity that will help you find levity. Embrace it as an activity that will be useful as you locate your wants. Embrace this exercise as an activity that silences the critic, if only for a few minutes.

TAKEAWAYS

- Over-the-top daydreams sneak past the critic.
- Daydreams help us discover our wants, which are windows into our souls.
- You have the power to daydream, and it's time to use it for positive purposes.

Donna has a problem. She never listens to herself. She talks and she talks and she talks, but she never listens. Her words seem to have no meaning. They are a running commentary of what she thinks, but rarely does she stop to hear her actual words and gauge their effect on her. She feels like she is not heard, and her running commentary is her way of asserting herself. She senses that her life could be better, but she doesn't know how to break out of the cycles she is in.

Donna is stuck in the persona she adopted to keep the critic quiet. She is literally drowning out her critic with her own talking, but the talking isn't productive or helpful to her. She could benefit from a practice of micro-meditations, spread throughout her day, to help her quiet her mind and find her connection with her own inner knowing.

Day 26

INTUITIVE NEXT ACTIONS

As we wrap up our time together, we have cleanup work to do. That's because if you have done the exercises that I laid out each day, then you have loose ends. You're likely wondering, *How often do I do the clearing work in order to gain benefit? How long do I keep up with the logbook? When do I stop using affirmations?*

The answers, as always, lie within you.

Our goal has been to help you break free from the critic so your authentic spirit can take up more space in your life, to guide you. To show you what excites you, what interests you, and what calls you forward in life. We want you to rely on that inner wisdom to decide what practice or exercise to do going forward.

My own personal routine is that I write, for myself, every day. This helps me air out my thinking and see things in new ways. I use affirmations and intentions. I have a default practice of noticing and saying what I want. I keep up with my logbook on most days. And I clear my mind when I feel uncertain, uneasy, or confused. I don't schedule these things. I just do them as they feel good or necessary to me.

Learning to lead an intuitive life is like winning a lottery that you didn't even know was available to you. You didn't enter, you didn't buy a ticket, and you didn't know it could change your life. For the better. I was previously someone who planned out her life and then executed the plan. Now I am someone who creates a plan to quiet my mind, and then I toss the plan in the trash. Here is why that works.

Project plans are ideas of how we think our projects, and our lives, should go. They are based on our limited minds and what we know, today, about the available paths to get us where we want to go. They are a great way to spend half an hour, having fun creating a road map. They are even helpful when they cause you to see a limiting belief.

Beyond that, however, project plans are mere fiction, and it's time to treat them that way.

Here is why: the critic sees your project plan and thinks, *This is the only way for us to get from point A to point B. This is the only way for us to accomplish our goal. This is the only way for us to improve our lives.*

The critic is narrow and rigid, whereas the true you is open and expansive. The true you sees many paths, lots of fun along the way, and destinations that are moveable. She sees infinite possibilities and solutions at every turn. She sees far more than you do. And she is your intuition.

Intuition is nothing more than an inner knowing. It presents to me as an idea of what I want to do. It presents to me often as an urge to move, to go into another room, or to simply walk around. It presents to me inspiration, which I then harness to take big action. And it's available to everyone if you want to tune in.

I see intuition as my spirit, guiding me forward in life. I now see my intuition as my best asset. It gives me what I need in every situation. My job is to show up and tune in to the ideas that seem to propel me forward in life.

Intuition is based on love. As in, I would love to do that. I would be interested to pursue that. I want to go there. These are love-based statements that your intuition pumps out all day. This is why we developed a habit of saying *I want*, so we could better align with our own inner knowing. That's why we practiced a habit of noticing and staying open, so we can be ready to receive inspiration throughout our day. That's why we cleared out the critic, so our own spirit can come in to occupy the space left behind by the critic.

That's how I visualize these old critical thought patterns: as energy that is moving out of my experience. And once it moves, my true self shines through more clearly, more brightly, and with more power.

The more I made it a point to release my critic, the more I experienced strong intuitive hits. The more I practiced staying open and aware, the more I realized that I was being flooded with positive and loving feedback. The more I made it a point to practice new ideas around my worthiness, enough-ness, and state of being loved, the more I found myself experiencing those feelings daily.

Intuition, to me, is now how I navigate life. But I still make project plans for all my goals. Why? Because I have found that once I make the plan, my mind settles in and stops searching for the hows. The only hiccup is when the critic thinks the plan that you create is the only plan to follow.

What I teach, then, is this: get into a habit of making project plans and then trashing the project plans to see what life delivers.

Say you have a desire to move to a new home. You have acknowledged that want, daydreamed about that want, and are holding the want as the precious gift it is. You now, however, feel ready to act toward that want, and you aren't sure what to do. You sit down and you create a road map that has phases to it.

You could plan phase one as a time for gathering your specific requirements. You could create another phase for driving around neighborhoods and looking at houses. You could create a phase for saving money for the down payment. Whatever you think needs to happen to achieve your goal, write it out in the plan. Then, put the plan away.

This exercise has helped me launch my newsletter, launch a blog, write this book, and add in various other projects I enjoy. I even wrote a project plan for our latest vacation and then put it away. I have seen this technique work countless times, so I am encouraging you to give it a try and to then use your intuition to help you achieve your goals.

What helps is to see the project plan as merely one path to get to my goal. One way through. One idea out of millions. I then allow my spirit to step in and guide me intuitively toward what I want, regardless of what the plan says. For instance, I created about twenty courses for my course catalog before I launched a single course. I intuitively felt in the flow in creator mode, so I kept creating, even though my critic was saying, *We have to get these courses packaged and ready to be launched.* Anytime I heard the words "have to," "must," and "should," I knew I was listening to the scared critic and made a conscious decision to tune out. Instead, I followed my intuition and kept creating.

The same was true for this book. Just when I began to launch my courses, the idea for this book was born. It came to me via my intuition, and it felt like a compelling idea, calling me forward. This was a complete pivot from the plan I had made, which had me getting all my coursework finalized and available for sale. Yet I could not deny the pull of this book, so I began placing more and more energy in the book-writing process.

Our minds only see what they can see. Our spirits, however, have access to far more information. That's how I experience it. As if someone with more power than me has a better idea than me, and my job is to follow my interests, wants, and passions to see where they take me.

Even with my complete faith in my intuition, I still make project plans. They feel essential to me because they help me create a belief that my goal is possible. They help me see that a path exists, and thus, I can relax and enjoy the ride. They help me get out of my head and into my intuition.

Intuitive work feels like me having a fun and productive day. It can also involve me having low energy, honoring that, and chilling out. But increasingly, I have days when my energy feels high, I feel connected, and I get a lot accomplished.

If I were still listening to the critic, here is what I would think: *Why did you just stop working and go search for an outfit online? Why did go chat with that coworker and waste twenty minutes? Why did you eat that?*

If you watched me work, you'd think I was forcing myself to sit for hours and write, but here is the truth: I can write for hours and feel like every minute is fun. I can edit my work for hours and get more and more excited about it. I can hold my writing for months without taking any action on it and know that someday I will know where it goes. And I got here honoring my wants and following my intuition.

Often, we see people who are highly productive and think, *I need to copy what she does. If she writes for hours, then I need to write for hours. If she does her own editing, then I need to do the same.* What we miss, however, when we seek to copy another's routine, is that we can't know their motivation. We can't know their intent. We can't know whether they are forcing themselves to work or enjoying the work they are doing.

I have a low tolerance for work I don't enjoy. I do my best to avoid it. Instead, I continually lean into projects, next actions, and work that satisfies me, and I let my days take care of themselves.

My intuition causes me to take new routes home, causes me to notice ads that hold appeal to me, and helps me see what next action calls to me. I stay open and aware of my thoughts and see thoughts as inspiration. When a thought recurs for me, I sit with it to understand its message. I try to notice how it makes me feel and whether it's a thought I need to change. I also notice whether it's a thought that excites me and calls me forward.

You are the best driver for your life. Not your critic. You are best cast in the lead in this production that is your life. You, and you alone, are the only person who has access to your superpower of intuition.

That's how I see intuition: as a message meant only for me. As guidance that tells me where to go next but is not leading anyone else. As an inner knowing that comes to me, for me, and helps me see everyone else as having the same access to their own inner knowing.

You, too, can lead an intuitive life. It doesn't take away from your analytical side; it enhances it. It doesn't make you soft or a pushover; it makes you strong and confident. It doesn't cause you to lose your goals; it helps you find new ways to accomplish your goals.

Which, to me, is the absolute best part of a spirit-led life. You draft the project plan as a way of saying, *Here is one route.* Then you put that plan away with a little prayer: *Show me the best route for me. Show me the route with the most surprises. Show me the way that creates the most fun.* Then, you sit back and let your days come to you, working always in the day you are in and with a strong connection to your intuition.

Intuitive working takes a little practice, but I bet you are better at it than you think. Here's why: your inner wisdom has always been there. It was simply being ignored because you thought the critic was your best guide for life. Turn the tables on the critic by setting this intent: *I intend to listen only to the true me as I make all my life decisions.*

TAKEAWAYS

- Project plans are a fun way to plan but not your best way to work.
- Intuitive next actions get you moving toward your goals and enjoying the journey too.
- Your intuition is always there for you.

Bill never gets a break. His life has been an endless loop of self-defeating habits, and he can't seem to stop them. He tries every diet, reads every self-help book, and sets new goals every year, but he never gets far. His own willpower always fails him, and he has no belief in his own ability to honor a commitment to himself. He feels that he has potential but that he can't improve himself until he drops the weight and gets his life in order. He's stuck and not sure where to turn.

Bill has a critic who not only is creating self-defeating habits but also criticizing Bill for those habits. It's a double whammy of a critic. Bill would benefit from building up his self-esteem and his belief in himself, through practicing affirmations and working to incorporate those into his life, so he can stand up to the critical thought patterns that hold him back.

Day 27

ART OF ALLOWING

To put a bow on all we have learned together, I am providing one final exercise that I find to be helpful for navigating life intuitively. It's a technique I use when I feel like I don't know which way to turn or what to do next. It's a way to help me open my mind to possibility when my mind is saying, *We have to work hard to accomplish our goals.*

This technique, which I call "turning over for handling," is where I sit, quiet my mind, and allow all my morass of thinking to come forward. I just sit with it. My chatter about all I must get done today. My worry about whether I will be successful in my goals. My mind running amok with mixed-up ideas and limiting beliefs. I sit, and I simply allow that chatter to occur. And then, I sit with awareness and say, *I turn this all over for handling to a power higher than me.*

It's an advanced way to deal with your critical thinking and requires that you practice a habit of not engaging or getting caught up in worry or negative thinking. It requires that you sit with that thinking, however, and let it simply be. I see it as a toddler who is having a tantrum. I let the tantrum run its course, and then I turn it over for healing.

That's what true healing is to me: trading in your negative thinking for better thoughts. Trading in your limitations for broad, expansive beliefs. Trading in your critic for a supportive and loving voice helping you succeed.

To achieve this state, you will need a practiced habit of meditation. A practice where you sit in stillness and allow thoughts to come and go without following them down the road. I am not saying you must be perfect in your meditation, but I am suggesting that a practice of doing this makes it much, much easier.

Sit in a comfortable spot and let yourself get centered on the inside. I like to hold my awareness in my core and be there as a way of saying, *I am here*. I run my tiny elevator down into my belly and sit there. My heart is open, and my awareness is free of any thought. In that space, I notice a tension. It feels like a pull or a push of energy. I allow it to be whatever it is, and then, as it reaches a place of built-up tension, I let it go. I surrender it. I turn it over for healing.

The practice, which feels to me like a clearing, is the natural result of a practice of being open. The more I tried to simply stay open, the more I experienced these floods of incoming tension and then a complete easing of the tension. Like waves of energy passing through me. And to me, it was a turnover of whatever I thought so it could become something better.

We are each creating thoughts all the time. It can't be stopped. But it can be slowed so you become more discriminating in what you think. As you do the exercises in this book, you are engaging in a full-frontal attack on the critic, which is what you need to start the process. At some point, however, you will move into a place of allowing, and this technique will take you home.

Allowing, to me, is a recognition that I am helped, assisted, and guided by spirit. Allowing is my way of saying, *I bet someone with a divine mind has an even better project plan than the one I cooked up.* Allowing is what I do when I feel stuck.

Feeling stuck is when you realize that you have taken this book and all its exercises as far as you can go, and you're ready to allow in help. That's what the stuck feeling is. A cue that you could turn it over and let the issues be resolved for you. I know this goes against everything our can-do and hardworking culture says, but it's a technique I have found success with.

When I turn it over, with intention, I free myself from worry. When I turn it over, with a positive expectation of a good result, I relax into the present moment and allow life to be what it is. When I turn it over, I am not abdicating my responsibilities; I am seeking help to grow.

There is no doubt in my mind that I am guided each day toward my highest purpose. Even if I can't see or know exactly what that purpose is. I simply know that by being me and expressing as my true self, I somehow take my place in the universe and fulfill my contract. And the way I access my path is to allow the path to be revealed to me.

Just five years ago, I had no plans to write a book. Just three years ago, I was struggling in recovery from a highly traumatic event. Just one year ago, I had no newsletter, no blog, and no plan to write this specific book. Yet here I am today, following my heart and doing what I love, all because I made a practice of allowing instead of controlling.

When my critic flares, I now sit with all that chatter and allow it, knowing that it will move through me quickly if I allow it.

Allowance comes to me in waves. When I work intuitively, I follow my inspiration and do what feels good to me. When I reach a point where I feel stuck, or unsure, I move into a practice of allowing and see what happens next. What this feels like to me is extreme productivity, punctuated with pauses where I clear in allowance.

I also use this practice at my job. When issues or problems present themselves to me, I sit with them and let all my worry, fears, and negative thinking come forward. How we will fail. How we already screwed up. How there is no path toward fixing the problem I was just presented with. I allow all that energy to come forward, and then I turn it over to be healed. After that, I find a sense of calm. I find that I get inspired to act on new ideas and solutions. I find that I have an urge to collaborate with certain people or bring them in on the problem-solving. I find that my intuition helps me find the easiest and shortest path out of the morass once I turn it over.

Allowance is but one tool in the tool kit for life. This book is filled with many tools, and only you will know which tool works best for you, based on where you are today. See this book as a smorgasbord of options that you can return to, over and over, when you need a little help. Simply open the book to a page and read, and you'll be on a path toward another solution to help you navigate life.

If you find a tool that is working, keep at it. If you find an exercise that makes you feel good, do it every day. If you find anything that eases your tension, add it to your life with a firm intention to lose your connection to fear so your established connection to love can blossom.

Allowance, for me, is a tool I turn to when I am uncertain. I see uncertainty as the time before I become certain, and allowance helps me navigate uncertainty with ease. We all have times when life feels murky, or when we are not yet at our goals. Use that time to engage in a process of allowance, and see your goals come to you more quickly.

Once you turn your attention away from pushing your way to your goals, life seems to help you find ways to allow in that which you want. We hear of examples of this all the time. The couple that becomes pregnant once they stop trying. The person who finds true love once they stop looking and simply love themselves. The project that came to completion once you withdrew your attention from it. These, to me, are all reinforcing what I have experienced. When I pull my attention away from efforting and into allowing, I move through change more quickly.

That's what a goal is. You changing yourself, your life, or your surroundings, in order to feel better. By allowing, you make that change more quickly.

Which is why allowing is so helpful for those of us who want to lose the critic. Our first step was to do the work of clearing our own blocks, in an aware sort of way. Then we put the focus on our wants, which are powerful activators. And now it's time to move into allowance, as a way of saying, *I could use help in cleaning up these thought patterns for good.*

Your life is about to change for the better if you allow it. Your life is about to become more fun if you allow it. You are about to fall in love—with yourself—all over again if you allow it.

I see allowance as the tool that I reach for last, once I have done my part. I see it as a gift of spirit that helps me turn my critical and negative thinking into positive and objective thinking. It helps me see in a more neutral way, at first, and then in a more loving way after that. From negative to neutral to positive. Over and over.

Which begs the question of whether we could all simply allow and be healed? Truth be told, I am not sure. Some part of me sees that as a path. But here is what I have found, based on my personal journey. I needed to show up and own my creation of the critic to stop my thought patterns from repeating. I needed to do the work of clearing out my limiting beliefs that kept the critic alive. I needed to see and understand why I had allowed the critic to run my life so that I didn't fall back into a cycle of that way of living. And once I was ready to let go of the critic for good, my practice of allowance took me home.

TAKEAWAYS

- You don't have to go it alone; you can ask for help.
- Allowance is one way to allow help to find you.
- Turning it over to your spirit is always a good idea.

Adam is full of self-confidence, but he is always chasing something new. He loves the thrill of a new project, a new job, or even a new love interest. He knows that he could settle down and do life as others do it, but anytime a new idea catches his attention, he runs toward it. He doesn't see this as a problem, but he knows that others do, particularly his parents. Adam does his best to settle down and stay stable, but the lure of something new and different always calls to him.

Adam has a healthy relationship with his critic and would do well to give himself space from those who have different ideas of what his life is supposed to look like. Adam could use any of the exercises in this book to bolster his belief that he, and he alone, is the best judge of a life well lived, and those exercises would give him the freedom he seeks.

Day 28

SOOTHING SELF-TALK

My process for writing this book was intuitive and self-paced. I showed up each day and did the work that came to me. The work I felt inspired to do that day. The work that seemed interesting to me. If I didn't have time to write, or didn't feel inspired to write, I skipped the day and made sure to tell myself that skipping a day was fine. It was my way of staying ahead of the critic and keeping myself soothed.

When our children were young, my husband and I used the cry-it-out technique to allow our kids to teach themselves to self-soothe. We used the practice judiciously and only when we felt like they were ready and capable to soothe themselves back to sleep in the middle of the night. It was hard, at times, to hear them cry, but the results we saw in their behavior and in their sleeping made it clear to us that we were right to help them learn to self-soothe.

It's time for you to learn how to self-soothe so you can keep the critic at bay.

To do this, you self-soothe before the critic shows up. You use your own self-talk and words to create ideas of success before the critic shows up and tells you what a mess you've made. Be so proactive that the critic is going to fall silent anytime you get ahead of it.

With your new awareness and skill of noticing, be prepared for your triggers. If you beat up on yourself when you don't exercise, then turn your focus on self-talk that combats that cycle. If you feel tense or low because you didn't work hard enough today, then get ahead of that cycle with practiced self-talk. And if you are hard on yourself because you aren't nice enough or good enough, then build up new ideas that help you fight back from those judgments.

Only you know your triggers. For some, a trigger could be a person who slights or disrespects them. For another, a trigger could be their feelings of inferiority around wealthy people. Still others are triggered by people in power. And still others are triggered every time they eat.

Triggers are nothing more than trip wires that exist within us and are meant to be early-warning signs. Start today by noticing what triggers send you into a criticism cycle. Know them, out them, and then proactively get ahead of them. With your words.

If you know you are triggered when you eat something deemed unhealthy by the powers that be, then use a practice of saying, *It's OK to eat this. I am perfectly safe. I know what is best for me.* If you are triggered by someone commenting on your appearance, then swoop in and say, *I like how I present; I am proud of how I look; I dress to satisfy me and no one else.* If you have a trigger around being told what to do at work, practice saying, *I am in charge of me, and I have chosen this job because I want the pay; I am in charge of what I think.*

Self-soothing is a personal responsibility. I find that it works best when I talk out loud. I frequently walk and talk to myself to build up the messages I need to hear on the subjects where I know my inner dialogue skews negative. (Thank God for earbuds, which make it look like I am on a call.) At first, I had to practice saying these messages every day, but now I can sense when I have tripped a trigger and need to self-soothe.

You will get triggered, and you will fall back into your old patterns. On occasion. And in that moment, you will reach for and find words to self-soothe as a way of keeping the critic from taking over and taking you down a rabbit hole of negative thinking.

We all do this. We make up stories around what others think of us. We create tales around how we were slighted or left out. We tell ourselves that we didn't succeed because we were never meant for success. Your work is to catch this negative thinking, pull yourself out of the downward spiral, and then self-soothe with your words.

If you are spinning a tale of how your friends never text you, tell a tale that flips the script and says that your friends all love you and will seek you out when they are ready. If you are engaging in thought spirals over a problem at work, talk yourself through a solution that comes in just when you need it most. If you are spiraling out of control with ideas of how you screwed up, stop and tell a story of how you succeeded.

Self-talk is a daily ritual I engage in. If you get good at this, you can talk your way through any stressful situation. You can stop negative thought patterns and ideas of unworthiness with ease. You can, if you do this enough, build up an entirely new belief system that supports all your big goals.

Self-talk, to me, is the antidote to unaware thought patterns that buzz in the background of life. Self-talk is a tool that I always have access to. And self-talk can be fun.

I now self-talk my way to success. I talk about how I am crushing all my life goals. I talk about how I just had the best day of my life so far. I talk about how I am only getting better and better with age.

But I started with soothing self-talk to get over the critic. I often said, *I'm OK.* I repeated over and over, *There is nothing wrong with me.* I came back, again and again, to this: *I am safe.* I used words and messages I needed to hear to keep me from losing myself to the critical mind.

Our minds are not the problem. That they are unsupervised could be. It is only when we go unaware that our minds seem to veer off into a ditch of negative thinking. It is only when the mind is not made aware of this propensity that the cycle keeps repeating. The path forward then is to own up to the fact that our unsupervised minds need our supervision to help us be who we want to be.

Soothing self-talk is one way to repattern the mind toward what you want. Soothing self-talk could be as simple as saying *I am* when you feel undervalued. Soothing self-talk could be a practice of saying *I am worthy* and meaning it. Soothing self-talk could be a practice of saying *I am enough* every time you feel less than.

If you are new to this, start with simple statements. *I am. I am worthy. I am enough.* Add to that, *I'm OK. I am safe. I belong.* Build up to ideas that say, *I am good. I am loving. I am loved.* When you feel yourself being pulled into negativity, these ideas can keep you going and let all that negativity pass right by you.

Over time, you'll gain more awareness of your specific trip wires, and you can address them head-on. When someone disrespects you, you can say, *I am valued, heard, and appreciated.* When you are triggered by someone in power, you can say, *I am powerfully in charge of who I am.* When you feel tension because there is conflict in your life, you can detach and say, *I am free to disengage from this conflicting situation.*

What you will eventually see is this: your triggers provide you with exactly the words you need to self-soothe.

In fact, I now see that the situations that trigger me provide me the greatest opportunity for growth.

If I am strongly frustrated with a situation, I can see that there is a message I need to hear to pull me out of frustration. I find that message and give it to myself. If I feel anger or disappointment in others, I can see where I need to change my expectations and find peace. If I feel that another person is tormenting me, I can talk to myself and find my power to rise to the occasion.

Your self-talk is a powerful weapon. Use it to better your life. Use it to stay ahead of situations where you know you will be triggered.

If you know that going to the beach puts you into a spiral of body shame, practice body love before your toes hit the sand. If you know that new technologies or tasks make you feel tense, then use a running dialogue of how easy those activities are before you start. If you know you feel fear when you drive, create a self-talk routine of affirmations before you get in the car.

I have used this technique for big presentations, for work projects that felt overwhelming, and for writing this book. I took breaks and dealt with my anxiety as I wrote things that felt vulnerable, revealing, and hard for me. I talked myself through the sections that I felt were a little woo-woo and were a little too simplistic. When my mind wandered to the publication process, or even allowing another person to read this work, I self-talked my way into a place of peace and excitement for those next stages.

Self-talk is a balm that you can apply to any hurt. Self-talk is a process that you can use for any problem. Self-talk is going on in your head, right now, whether you are aware or not. Why not bring your awareness to your self-talk and heal yourself?

To take this one step further, write out practiced self-talk that hits your triggers head-on. Record yourself saying those words, and give yourself the gift of your own words as you drift off to sleep.

Triggers are designed to evoke emotion so that you know where to put your attention. Triggers bug us so we don't just pass by the trigger and leave that trip wire exposed. Triggers can be seen as valuable indicators of where your best path lies.

For me, my triggers caused me to get laser-focused on the soothing self-talk I needed. I had a habit, for years, of asking myself, *What's wrong with me?* It played in the background and was the basis for all my self-improvement forays. Once I finally saw that trigger, I began an aggressive practice of saying, *There is nothing wrong with me.* To this day, those six words bring me a sense of tremendous relief, and I use them any time life suggests that I need to change.

Your own words hold great power. Use them to build your platform of love. Use them to soothe your own wounds. Use them to help you move where you want to go.

TAKEAWAYS

- You can stay ahead of your critic by using soothing self-talk.
- Know your triggers and stay ahead of them.
- Use the power of your words to heal yourself.

Harry never believed that he could find a job that he loves, so he took the job that he felt made the most money. *If I am going to be miserable, I may as well make money*, he thought. Harry worked a long career, and retired with the plan to play more golf, travel, and sleep in. Once he retired, though, he found himself bored, listless, and not motivated. He found that, with all his free time, he was not motivated to do anything, which only upset him even more, as he felt like he was wasting his retirement. He consulted with his priest, who helped him find a volunteer opportunity, but Harry's heart wasn't in it, and he wasn't sure how to proceed.

Harry may be accustomed to working on other's priorities and not his own because he listened to a critic who said his priorities don't matter or aren't possible. As Harry reforms this idea, he will notice that his own desires and priorities come forward again, helping him live a more enriching life.

CONCLUSION

We started this book with one idea: that you could lose your critic and learn to trust yourself again. And that is the fundamental block that most of us carry that keeps us returning to the critic. We simply don't trust ourselves.

Yet trust doesn't come on the back of a wish and a prayer. Trust emanates from a conscious decision to show up for yourself, day after day, to do the work of undoing the patterns of thought that have held you hostage for years. The process of doing these exercises matters just as much as the results they bring you.

A commitment to yourself is the best commitment you can make. Once you establish a relationship of love and trust with yourself, you not only lose the critical impulse, but you gain a sense of self that is super-attractive. That is super-conductive. That is super-appealing.

The critic was the negative mindset. We cleared those blocks to allow you to adopt a neutral mindset, which then allowed you to move into a positive mindset. And a positive mindset holds great power.

A positive mindset can cause you to achieve more than you ever thought possible. A positive mindset can set you up to have good and great days, even when life swirls around you. A positive mindset can become a bridge of sorts between who you once were and who you truly are. A positive mindset is a superpower that you likely did not see coming.

Those of us mired in critic mentality think our critic is our superpower. That our hyperawareness of what is off, wrong, or out of line proves our value. Yet that thinking is outdated, antiquated, and of another era. This is the era when all things are possible. This is the time when we don't have to guard the rails but can move forward and soar. This is the time of the most freedom that we have ever experienced. And that's a genie you can't put back in the bottle.

Once you see, and then experience, the superpower of a positive mind, you will have little taste for going back to the critic mentality. Once you see how productive a person becomes once they are doing what they love, you lose the ability to work any other way. Once you see how much love you can put into the world by loving yourself, you will never self-denigrate again.

All true learning is experiential. I hope my words inspire you to experiment, to try, and to play with all the exercises in this book. Each one chips away at the foundation of the critic. Each one takes aim at the critic's infrastructure. Each one blows to bits the critic's reason for being.

What awaits you on the other side is a life full of days that you love. What is there for you is a 24-7 love spigot that is available for free. What you'll find is the path leads, over and over again, right back to you. The true you.

You don't create who you are. You become who you are meant to be. The critic is simply a barrier between the true you and the you who you think you are today. Take down that barrier, and the result is a freight train that can't be stopped. It's the power of your own soul expressing into your life, calling you toward people, experiences, and projects that you love.

I, too, am a work in progress. But I have endeavored to add in more and more of what I love to every day that I am alive. And the transformation in me has been material. My story, however, is not nearly as interesting to you as your story. Get interested in what you think. Get interested in what you love. Get interested in living life without the need for a critic. Do that, and your story will be written by your own spirit.

The path for each of us is bespoke. What I did, and what I learned, is offered here as a suggestion for how to lead your own inner transformational journey. You can tear down the walls. You can lose the critic. You can become more of your true self every day. How you walk that path, I am certain, will vary, but still I believe that we each have wisdom to share with one another.

If you want to join a community of like-minded souls who are each walking their own journey, head over to my website, where you will find ample opportunities to connect: SueErhart.com.

It has been my pleasure to write this book. It has been a project that has called me forward in a way that other projects have not. That's because there was a piece of me in each of the exercises I asked you to do. Now that we have ended our time together, I have one final ask: if you found this work helpful, drop me a note. I thrive from knowing that my words have helped others, a want that it took me a long time to acknowledge. Having acknowledged it, I now know that want holds an important clue for my life's journey.

You are ready to do this work on your own. You have all the answers you need inside you for a happy and awesome life. You have access to guidance that will show you the way. Tear down the critic and let that guidance emerge.

POSTSCRIPT

In the opening pages, I told you that the upshot of losing the critic was that your own, natural spirit swoops in to take up residence and begin to grow. Not that your spirit ever leaves you, but it helps if you see your spirit sprouting all around you as you do the work of losing the critic.

Our society has given us a word for the critic that includes the word *inner*. As you likely noticed, I have carefully extracted that word from discussion of the critic. Here is why: that one word causes many people to believe that the critic is their inner wisdom.

I touched on this briefly when I revealed that I thought my critic was my soul. I advocate that we drop the word *inner* from the idea of the critic. And begin, instead, to see the critic as a thought form that exists outside of us.

Those who tie the word *critic* to *inner* are well-intentioned. They mean to suggest that there are thoughts in your head that cause you to self-criticize. The part I want to emphasize is not the location of this critic, but the fact that the inner you—the true you—is always loving, interested, and wanting more. There simply is nothing to criticize once you align with your true self. You might compare yourself as a way of noting your differences, but you lose the taste for criticism.

What helped was to imagine myself removing the critic from my mind and then replanting in that space thoughts of love. Thoughts that said, *I love myself.* Thoughts that said, *I can achieve any goal I want.* Thoughts that said, *I am a powerful creator of the best life ever.* These ideas helped me blossom, even as the critic occasionally came barking at my door.

My work in kicking my critic out of my experience has been fully transformative. So transformative that most days, I forget what life was like when I was ruled by the critic. Which is one reason I write. It helps me to see my progression away from fear-based thinking, and toward love-based thinking.

The words *inner* and *critic* can be disassociated if you set that intent. I have, and I now see that my use of the term *inner critic*, in my past, made it difficult for me to shake the critic. Consider trying out this new idea: *the critic is not inside you*. It exists entirely as a figment of your mind.

The idea of the inner critic is something that I see talked about more and more. Those of us who have lived with a critic know that words matter, as they can cut us down or lift us up. See your own spirit rising from within to take up residence in you and around you, and see the critic being pushed farther and farther away, until you simply cannot hear the negative fear-based thinking anymore. It's a powerful visual that never ceases to uplift me.

Your critic will bark on occasion, but the more you set an intent to allow your own spirit to shine through, the less you will be bothered. Now, when I slip into a critical mindset, there's always a good reason, and I use the step backward to fortify myself for the road ahead. Not that life is hard, but because I want all parts of me along as I enjoy this new way of living.

What the critic gave me was the gift of contrast. I lived life with the critic, so I now enjoy the fresh sweetness of being critic-free. I now enjoy the power of harnessing my mind to accomplish anything I want. I now enjoy the total pleasure of living life on my terms instead of allowing the critic to guide my days.

How's that going, you ask?

Well, I wrote this book in under a month. I started a newsletter and a blog and have a suite of online courses that would be helpful to anyone who wants to uplevel their lives. I am happily married and loving life as a parent of teenagers. I am comfortable in my nine-to-five job as an executive at a large company and enjoy new challenges, new experiences, and new ideas. I am in love with myself and feel like I have a superpower that anyone could access if they wanted. And I have a strong sense of my spirit as my best guide for life.

All that simply from kicking my critic off its perch.

What I want you to know is this: your inner wisdom is wise beyond her years. Your inner voice is loving, kind, and fun. Your inner knowing is strong, confident, and sure. Your inner guidance is positive, exciting, and forward-looking. Your inner being is a bundle of energy waiting to escape once you fire the jailer that kept you small. Your critic has held you hostage, and it's time for you to set yourself free.

ABOUT THE AUTHOR

Sue Erhart is the creator of the popular platform, Practical Spirituality, where she writes about all manner of topic that affect our relationship with our true selves. Her work empowers her loyal readers who look forward to her weekly newsletters, filled with practical and useful advice for navigating your own spiritual journey.

Sue is also an executive at a large corporation, where she leads the areas of legal, compliance, risk management, and cyber security. She is a beloved boss, leader, and mentor, and her writing reflects her deep grounding in the working world.

Sue has a penchant for positivity that shines through her work. She is passionate about sharing her hard-earned lessons in life, as a way of saying, *I did it the hard way, but you don't have to*. She draws from her own experiences to show her followers an easier path.

Sue resides in Cincinnati, Ohio with her husband and two children. She's an avid cook, quilter, writer and lover of life. She loves to receive notes from readers and welcomes them to start their own spiritual journey at her website: SueErhart.com